THE

The Art of Joyful Living

JACQUES PEZÉ M.D.

AND

PETER ROCHE DE COPPENS PH.D.

ELEMENT

Rockport, Massachusetts ● Shaftesbury, Dorset

Published in the U.S.A. in 1991 by Element Inc, 42 Broadway, Rockport, MA 01966

Published in Great Britain in 1991 by Element Books Limited, Longmead, Shaftesbury, Dorset

This book is published in French under the title
L'ALTERNANCE UNE CLE ESSENTIELLE DE LA VIE
Editions de l'Aire, Lausanne, Switzerland
Text originally written in English translated by Sophie Ceyreste
Text originally written in French translated by Kenneth Holmes

Designed by Roger Lightfoot
Cover illustration 'Bird and Lilies' by Ginger Wilson of Mercury Designs
Cover design by Max Fairbrother and Barbara McGavin
Typeset by Burns & Smith Ltd., Derby
Printed and bound in the U.S.A. by Edwards Brothers Inc.

Library of Congress Cataloging–in–Publication Data

Pezé, Jacques, 1923–
    [Alternance, une cle essentielle de la vie. English]
    The art of joyful living : discovering the simple key of alternance/Jacques Pezé and Peter Roche de Coppens; translated from the French by Kenneth Holmes.
    Translation of : L'Alternance, une cle essentielle de la vie.
    1. Conduct of life.   2. Polarity (Philosophy)   3. Rhythm-
    -Psychological aspects.   I. Roche de Coppens, Peter.   II. Title.
    BF637.C5P4813   1991
    158'.1—dc20   91-26158

    ISBN 1-85230-272-0

British Library Cataloguing in Publication Data

A catalogue record for this book is available from the British Library

ISBN 1-85230-272-0

I dedicate this book to the memory of my father, Gabriel Pezé, philosophy master of the French Lycée in Beirut, and my mother Lucie Pezé, both of whom taught me to have the will to fight for an authentic life.

J.P.

This book is also dedicated to my beloved mother, Baroness Alice de Coppens, and to my father, Georges Roche, both of whom brought me into this world, who raised me and guided me during the stormy years of my youth and adolescence; who provided love, shelter, and emotional and existential security during W.W.II and the birth of a New Age of Humanity; and who allowed me to release and express my creative potential to become the person I am today. Together, they provided the major "Alternance" of unconditional and conditional love, of kindness and diplomacy together with rigor and firmness, which prepared me for the battles and the authentic rewards of human life. For this . . . and much more . . . they have my eternal Love and gratitude that human words fail to adequately express but which is manifested in my work and being.

P.R. DE C.

Acknowledgments

For their kind and invaluable help with rereading the typescript and bringing the various chapters into harmony, we must thank:

Monique Auberty, *Senior Lecturer at the University of Tours.*

Pierre Binet, *Honorary Professor of Literature.*

Catherine Brunet, *Mathematics Teacher.*

Benoît Lafleche, *President of the Geobiology Research Centre, Paris.*

Chantal Legoupil, *Senior Executive, France Télécom.*

Monique Mary, *B.Litt., Research Librarian.*

Gaston Moles, *Vice President of the Hahnemann Foundation for Medical Research.*

Anna Guellec, *Research Consultant (Ingenieur d'Etudes) in the Psychology Department of the Ecole Pratique des Hautes Etudes, Paris.*

Yann Pezé, *Science Student.*

Acknowledgments for North America:

Richard Payne, *Editor in Chief, Element, Inc.*

Robert Muller, *former Assistant Secretary General of the United Nations and now Chancellor of the United Nations University for Peace.*

James E. Gilbert, *Ph.D., President of East Stroudsburg University.*

Orest Bedrij, *President of Griffen Capital Management, internationally recognized Scientist and Author.*

David F. Copeland, M.D., *Allergist/Immunologist.*

Meera Sharma, M.D., *Rheumatologist.*

James E. Leiding, Ph.D., *Head of Sociology Department, East Stroudsburg University.*

I would also like here to express my special gratitude to Professor Arnold Kaufmann, the mathematician, with whom I discovered the fundamental principals of alternance.

I thank the physicians of the Société Française de Médecine Générale, among whom I worked for so long; also the physicians of the Fondation de Recherche Médicale Hahnemann who have enabled me to obtain concrete verification of certain application of the ALTERNANCE theory.

In brief then—

If you are weary, tired of life, emotionally depleted, intellectually or energetically stuck – ALTERNATE, i.e., do the opposite of what you have been doing but not for too long. It is this first ''success'' or ''gulp of psychic oxygen'', the living experience of alternance's possibilities, that will help you understand this book and give you the motivation needed to work with it.

Contents

Personal Statements

The essence of life is LOVE – of the Creator and Supreme Intelligence and of our fellow humans – which leads to the awakening of spiritual consciousness. The Art of Joyful Living revolves around someone to love, something to do which one enjoys, and hope in a better future. True wisdom is not "not making mistakes" but never giving up and stopping to learn.

Peter Roche de Coppens

Throughout my life as a doctor, I have closely observed the essential content of the "human mechanism" and tried to repair it to the best of my capabilities. In so doing, I have noticed that those who do sincerely wish to progress, to evolve, for both their own and everyone else's benefit, are often capable of prodigious things, sometimes even of miracles.

I am a great believer in the addition of individualities. The only way in which our present world will ever overcome its difficulties will be by the sum total of its individuals' actions, as each of them accomplishes "his or her own personal development."
   Everything which can add some element to individual balance is therefore contributing to the common balance and peace.

Jacques Pezé

Introduction

Our normal and natural inheritance is joy in life, the joy of inner being, the joy of living with others, and the joy of being alive on the earth at this time. How do we awaken to this rightful inheritance? One of the keys is found in the principle and practice of alternance. With this simple key we rediscover a movement – of mind, body, and spirit – a spontaneous movement so often seen in nature that, once it has become part of our conscious awareness, can vivify us and free us to enter more fully into the sacred dance of life.

In this book, translated from the French *L'ALTERNANCE: une cle essentielle de la vie*, we have kept the French term ALTERNANCE rather than its literal translation – alternation – because it has a smoother, more liquid, and life enhancing sound; also because it gives us a new term to introduce the new idea which is central to this book.

Alternance is a fundamental principle which is both simple and obvious. Because it is present both all around us in nature and within us, and within our essential movements, we can recognize and understand it with relative ease. Some examples of it are:

- inhalation/exhalation,
- heart rhythm: systole/diastole (contraction/dilation), and
- day/night.

It is the movement of the fundamental pendulum of creation, which we rediscover in our biological life. Furthermore, it is our anguish and our hope, our limitation and our extension, marking the passage of time and weaving the fabric of our existence.

Alternance should **normally** be a part of our daily lives and basic habits, a natural reference and guide to a joyful way of living.

However, the ways of modern life and our present living habits, very often at odds with nature, have conspired to destroy and deviate our natural rhythms of alternance.

Nonetheless, deep within us, this fundamental movement of alternance lies dormant, temporarily arrested, or out-of-sync. Being an essential part of our nature, it can be awakened and reset in joyful motion.

The task, then, is to find a language – signs, images, and symbols – capable of speaking to this dormant or paralyzed power of alternance.

Alternance is multi-faceted: It offers infinite access-points and contains numerous relay-processes, specific for each individual. For that reason, this book will focus more on its essential aspects, often stating and re-stating these in various ways, so as to help each person find the image or formulation which best speaks to his or her own unconscious.

Thus may the pendulum of alternation, that dynamic, time-integrating basis of life, so simple and robust, possessed by all, be reset in motion, and at just the right tempo. Learning once how to liberate its rhythms, we can then let its genius swing into action.

How To Use This Book

The usual way to read a book is to turn the pages, dutifully, one after the other; if that is what you are used to, then you will be surprised to find that this book is different. Already as a first practical lesson in alternance, we have varied the contents so that, without any formal logical progression, your subconscious can feel free to give one chapter preference over another. By discovering that particular chapter's meaning, your subconscious can move in a direct way to reanimate its rhythms, recover its vitality, and create for itself a new degree of freedom.

We not only want to tell you about alternance, but also want to help you put it into practice and this book, with its apparent suspension of formal order, has been written in such a manner as to straightaway give you that opportunity.

You can yourself take this element of variety, already present, much further by letting your imagination guide you into reading the chapters "according to your whim". This is precisely what we recommend you doing, each time that you feel in an innovative mood and ready to follow your impulse. That way of reading will give your intuition the best possible chance of coming into play – and developing intuition is what we want to encourage as much as possible. The progress you thus make will be spontaneous, rarely logical, and generally uncalculated. This new way of discovering natural rhythms is a little like jumping into the sea, more in the spirit of splashing about, enjoying its invigorating freshness, than in swimming a methodical crawl or in training in hopes of placing first in competition.

The conception and structure of this book intends this sort of reading. Don't be afraid to take advantage of it, or to use this artistic license in reading, in every which way, according to your impulses.

There is no risk that you will miss the part that might be vital for you: trust that you will discover that passage automatically. The essential points are, in fact, made again and again in different ways and you cannot fail to find them.

Above all else, bear in mind that this book has not been written primarily to give you knowledge but to give you movement. This is why movement is part of the structure itself: an alternance between two authors, between different levels of awareness (conscious, subconscious, and supraconscious), and between contributions from tradition, science, and everyday life.

That then is another way of using this book. However, in undertaking this joyful ''aeration of your subconscious'', if you can avoid the trap of linear logic, you will obtain quicker results and have the sensation of a new, re-found breath.

We also provide, in an appendix, a technical reference for specialists, indicating why and how this book has been constructed.

Foreword

In reading this book, some readers might be astonished by:

- the absence of classical layout, consisting of a logical progression of ideas: theory, counter-theory, synthesis, and final conclusive summary,
- a seeming disorder, and
- repetitions.

Habitually, we expect a structured theme – yet one more to add to our accumulated knowledge. Our goal in writing this book has been to try to bring about the opposite: something which will unclutter the mind and give it space and allow it more ease in its movements.

As far as we are concerned, it is not a question of adding to the furniture of your conscious mind but of multiplying the possibilities which can liberate your unconscious mind and get it successfully unstuck. The natural consequence of this should be a happy and **spontaneous** improvement in your conscious and subconscious relations.

Actually, there is a layout, a plan. We will discuss it at the end of the book, in the technical appendix. We would ask you not to bother about that right now and not to read it before you have benefited "un-calculatingly" from the natural stimulations which can come in a straight reading of the text. The layout does not tally with the logical workings of the conscious but with the more particular demands of the unconscious mind. More will be said about this later.

As for repetitions, they are useful for two reasons: First, we want each chapter to be capable of being read in isolation and to provide something whole in itself. Therefore you can start reading almost anywhere you fancy, then stop and pick up the threads again at any time. You are tied to nothing. We have avoided any "ensnaring identification". We do not ask you to accept any particular theory; only to allow the possibility within yourself of a new vitality.

Secondly, repetition is not necessarily something to be shunned when embodying fundamental, creative, and formative ideas, where the whole point is that they really sink in. Otherwise what can one say of prayer or about the proverbs, which one repeats over and over again?

Remember that this book has not been written to increase the volume or quantity of your knowledge and your wisdom but, before anything else, dear reader, to help you feel more at ease with yourself, happier, more open to life's joys, its rhythms, and more capable of spontaneous creativity.

The Basis of Alternance

Alternance in the Plant Kingdom

Fixed to the soil out of which they grow, plants experience an external alternance and react to it in situ. The major alternances they are subject to are:

Day/Night

This controls their respiratory rhythm. During the day, green plants absorb carbon dioxide and give off oxygen; during the night, the process is reversed. (Because of this some say it is not wise to have plants in bedrooms, but they may be confusing carbon dioxide, which is non-toxic, with carbon monoxide which is highly toxic.) Some flowers, morning glories and day lilies, for instance, open during the day and close at night, and some vice versa – for example, the fragrant night-blooming jasmine.

The Seasons

Each spring, young shoots emerge and sap rises; plants are reborn. Summer expands and blooms into ripeness and maturity. With autumn comes the harvest and the winding down of the cycle, a sort of old age. In the cold stillness of winter's earth, the seed lays dormant; above ground if the cold is extreme, some plants may die, others surviving only through a few scraps of root. With spring, once again, the cycle commences.

Heat/Cold

Some plants, like bulbs and perennials, require a period of cold in order to flower in the warm weather. Temperature changes in the spring affect the flow of sap, especially the delicious sap of the maple which is made into maple syrup.

Humidity/Dryness

This alternance is most vividly seen in the desert. When it rains on the dry earth of the desert, the formerly arid ground covers itself with vegetation with remarkable rapidity. When drought follows, the only plants to survive are those with impermeable leaves or those that have become prickly, like the cacti.

Alternance in Animals

Animals alternate: it is one of the prime characteristics of their way of life. Unlike plants, they are not fixed to one place and their mobility means that natural alternances are not so implacably imposed on them. They can react by shifting place, taking shelter, shivering or running to get warm when it is cold, or sleeping in a shady place or on cool tiles when it is very hot.

The Basic Day/Night Alternance

Animals do have this basic alternance – even glowworms, who have their own torches. It is actually quite funny to see chickens take themselves to bed as the sun sets. When an eclipse occurs and the sunlight disappears unexpectedly and rapidly, any cock who takes his job seriously will busily usher the hens back to the hen-house to sleep for the night. Hangers-back receive severe pecks. Then, the eclipse over and daylight returning, all the hens flap about and leave their perches as if a new day had come. The particular cock that I observed once in these circumstances seemed to be gravely worried about the functioning of his own personal clock. In a great fluster of agitation and perplexity, he nevertheless – and, in fact, more than ever – maintained his role as leader of the hens.

The Seasons

Many animals (dormouse, badger, bear, hedgehog, bat, etc.) hibernate for the winter. Marmots choose a sheltered spot and sleep there for months on end. The tortoises disappear from my garden, buried in the earth until spring. Alpine animals descend, either of their own accord or led by men, from their peaks to the more clement valleys below. Birds migrate across oceans and continents, returning to former breeding grounds or in search of a better climate.

The Tides

This is a phenomenon of remarkable amplitude, based on the phases of the moon. My cocker spaniel could sense the moment when the tidal movement was changing and the tide was about to come in. Becoming very worried once, he ran back up shore, yapping at me to follow: I was blissfully unaware of the tidal shift and could well have been caught by the rapid inrush of the tide.

The Human World

Mankind's Loss of Alternance

Our loss of a natural and normal alternance is fairly recent, occurring within the last century. Before then, most of the essential alternances still existed as the rhythms of human life were still closely tuned to those of nature and the agricultural cycles.

Everyone moved about either by horse or on foot and so the daily physical exertion must have been considerable. No one needed an imitation bicycle in their bathrooms for exercising, sweating and getting out of breath by pedaling in the same place in order to go nowhere. The body/mind alternance had much less chance of going off course.

The Loss of Day and Night. If we consider this loss starting with the discovery of fire, still man with his torches and, later, candles could only in a very limited way break through the vast, dark shades of night. Darkness remained omnipresent, impenetrable, and obligatory as long as the sun stayed hidden. No one could escape the basic day/night alternance.

It is only relatively recently that we have been able to confound day with night, and night with day, to the point where around the clock production schedules, media broadcasts, and even artificial lighting used to regulate plant and animal growth are the norm. In the wake of this has come a profound disorientation – there are more and more people who say they no longer know how they live.

The Loss of the Holy. This is another recent turn of events. For thousands of years the sacred and its associated rituals have been part of human individual and communal life, bringing an alternance between the ordinary and the extraordinary, between the mundane perception of daily life and an enlarged vision offering another perspective on our human experience.

In the developing scientific age, mankind lost its sense of the sacred; at the same time modern man discovered in-depth psychology and distinguished different levels of the mind. Taking research and rational analyses further and further, we somehow lost the overview in the process. As a reaction to this over-accentuation of analysis, today we see the emergence of the wholistic approach. This is the current wave breaking around us, bringing with it no small amount of confusion.

Anti-alternance Gadgets. We live in an age that has developed great ingenuity in the art of making people lazy. Ups and downs are cushioned and finger-tip controlled, ameliorated and placated; one fairly floats on the airbed of life, stretched out and full-bellied, safely ensconced in the certainty that nothing too disagreeable can happen.

Air conditioning (wrongly called in French, by some quirk of language, climatization) means there is always the same regulated air to breathe, and so we are without the stimulation needed to trigger a reflex response – and reflexes are much in need of alternance for their constant reanimation.

Instant food and the "burger" life: Around the clock one can drive through any number of fast food drive-ins and order breakfast, lunch, or dinner, perhaps eating it on the way to work or some pressing appointment. At home, what used to be a relaxing time to savor the smells and aromas of food being prepared has now been curtailed by the advent of the microwave oven. For exhausted working mothers, let us admit, these can be helpful at times, but at what loss to the rhythms of human ingestion and digestion?

American supermarkets abound now in freeze-dried instant soups, instant rice, microwave instant entrees, and for dessert, a 5 minute "microwavable" cake mix. Yet this gimmickry and gadgetry does not "flavor enhance" the essential mediocrity of this food, any more than it truly nourishes; it remains tasteless behind the packaged illusion of variety.

Excessive comfort and excessive softness: The over-padded life is the natural extension of the now frequently encountered over-padded body in Western society. It becomes harder and harder to bother with bus and train schedules, much less walk to a depot or station, when a car is available, especially a car with roomy, plush, adjustable seats, multi-directional heat and air-conditioning, its own compact disc player, and telephone. It is hard to take the stairs or walk from the front door of the airplane terminal when others are gliding past on escalators and conveyor belts. Once on board, it is hard to resist the endless round of drinks, meals, magazines, music, and movies brought to us by a smiling hostess. Throughout modern life, we are encouraged and inclined to feel that discomfort is somehow unjust, something to be avoided at all costs, rather than something to be experienced, worked through, and overcome.

Home office machines: With the increasing use of home computers, printers, copy and fax machines in the home office we are discovering that machines do not necessarily afford us more leisure but now offer us the chance to work around the clock. With no escape from the demands of constant work, we lose yet more of the possibility for a natural alternation between work and rest.

Television and VCRs: With an ear and eye to worldwide current events at all hours of the day and night, with a satellite dish, perhaps, or cable or pay TV, the viewer, after the hefty task of sorting out what is available, has difficulty in freeing himself from this deluge of news and entertainment. Media overload sets in.

Of all forms of living being, only man is capable of opposing alternance, either by failing to acknowledge it or by refusing to accept it, inventing and saturating his life with ever more powerful and more sophisticated gadgets.

In what amounts to a campaign against alternance, it is only recently that man has been able to really and truly block off so many basic alternances to the point that he finds the very balance of his life is threatened.

Historical Perspective and Definition

Historical Perspective: The Loss of Alternance

In the dawn of time, human beings lived amid vast nature, an immensity of forests, plains and mountains. Life must have been almost entirely concerned with physical survival, finding food and protecting oneself from the elements, animals, and other human beings.

Yet for all their hardships, our ancestors' conscious life and behavior were balanced by an alternance which was unconscious, instinctive and **very alive**. Whenever they emerged from their abodes they were faced with an enormous external diversity which invigorated them with its vivid multiplicity, an intermingling of sensation, impulse, emotion, thought, imagination, will, sounds, and smells. Life was an intense mixture of needs to be satisfied and dangers to be faced; a mixture of what we might today refer to as "the outer world and the inner world", introversion and extroversion.

In time, humanity gradually drew further from nature to create society. In so doing, many instincts and impulses began to atrophy as we developed the power of reason, intelligence, and culture. Human beings lost a host of opportunities for instinctive and automatic alternance.

Modern society has favored mental development and, particularly in the West, has nurtured a "dictatorship of reason". This has given rise to unrestrained competition and a passion for success, to secure material well-being no matter what the price – but the price has been the loss of instinctive, spontaneous alternance; an alternance which nature seems to have envisaged so clearly in setting us as instinctual beings within the whole panoply of our varied and reactive environment.

This loss, in its turn, has brought about all sorts of illness and afflictions which modern medicine often finds hard to understand and cannot always cure for, even if we do manage to eliminate the symptoms in one area, lo and behold, they appear almost immediately in some other area or in some other way! This situation has reached such a point of aberration that one formula for healing people often prescribed today is no more than a minimum of essential alternances.

Right now, the very first thing to do is to make a conscious effort to **become aware** of the fact that the law of alternance is a fundamental principal for ensuring good health and staying in good working order. In former times that knowledge would have been there instinctively, as a basic part of our lives. In order to do this we need to awaken and develop our intuition. It will help us achieve a rhythm of alternance, indicating **when to alternate**, **in what way**, and **to what degree**.

People often get confused between instinct and intuition. Instinct is what has been handed down to us through our zoological heritage. Intuition is something which emerges from our faculties of supersensory perception. The difference must be stressed: one would not say that an animal has intuition because it is something proper only to humans.

Let us start by seeing the basic nature of alternance. Alternance is to be found wherever there is life, movement, and consciousness. It means **change**, the swing between a thing and its opposite, between hot and cold, day and night, between two different polarities, between the feminine and the masculine, between the happy and the sad.

Potentials for alternance exist between the creator and the created, the finite and the infinite, mind and matter, macrocosm and microcosm. We can discover one of the roots of the idea in the vision of Heraclitus, a Greek philosopher from the 5th century B.C.:

"All things change, move, and are transformed."

"One can never step in the same river twice."

"Grass and the philosopher's beard are growing while he contemplates the problems of the universe."

This already gives us a clue that the principle of alternance, which is primarily movement, is to be found reflected and echoed under a thousand varied guises in the cosmos and in nature, playing an immutable role in both.

Definition of Alternance in Daily Life

The basic idea is simply this: to periodically and systematically switch to doing *the opposite of what we have been doing*. And to do this at ever deeper, more conscious, and more refined levels. This implies the awakening and use of intuition – so we will know exactly when to alternate. Once we are in the habit of alternating at the right time, we need to learn how to alternate to the right degree, i.e., not too little, not too much.

One immediately sees there are infinite possibilities of alternance existing in very elemental ways in our daily lives.

In other times it was our robust life-forces and instincts which led us automatically and inevitably to alternate at just the right time and to just the right degree. Nowadays, having let our instincts atrophy and thus being cut off from our body's wisdom, we must instead use reason and knowledge (as well as awakened intuition) to animate a healthy alternance in our being and daily life.

Here, every individual must learn to know himself or herself, to heed themselves, managing their own life-objectives by using multiple alternances at different moments and on different levels. For example there is movement/rest, standing/sitting or reclining, light/shade, heat/cold, dryness/humidity, hardness/softness, inside/outside, windows open/windows closed, feeding/fasting, etc. Each of these little switches, these minor alternances, can liven us up.

In fact, what is alternance if none other than a becoming-conscious of the enormous inner richness we possess, then arousing it and actualizing our latent potential – an inner abundance which contains the fundamental movements of our life's powerful undercurrents?

A human being is a microcosm, an "enormous little universe" that is extraordinarily complex. Through alternance, one can vivify and express the remarkable wealth constituted by that microcosm's different dimensions, energies, vibrations, and varied faculties. In so doing we avoid blockage, a congealing of the inner life-force that comes from only nourishing one part of our being, which is multi-dimensional and greatly diversified.

That is how we can avoid the well-known error of mistaking a part for the whole (this error is called, in religion, "idolatry"); thereby we will not always move monodirectionally, letting certain parts of our being create a monopoly, or allowing them to become overdeveloped while ignoring others, in particular, stressing reason to the exclusion of intuition.

Alternance, then, forms part of the great law of harmony and "the sacred dance of life", both of which invite our participating in the Whole. Alternance does this by creating adept relationships between our conscious Ego and those aspects of existence which are of a far more vast and more complex nature; then, with this enlarged consciousness, we can learn to be more open to the unconscious.

In Our Difficult World: Alternance in Daily Life

Some aspects of our present-day world situation are quite marvelous and reveal astonishing progress. However, sociologists recognize the threats which we all see building up, perils which are also part of our new world, global ecological and economic problems, loss of the traditional family structure and function, and, more fundamentally, loss of a traditional criteria upon which to base judgment.

For a large number of people this is destabilizing: They no longer know quite who or what to put their trust in, and they feel ill at ease, worried, and more or less out-of-phase, either ahead of or lagging behind the times in which they live.

Within this difficult world, as traditional values crumble but rigidity and blockages multiply, where most of us no longer have clear feelings about what is the norm or what we can cleave to, or what we can use to overcome our problems, there is still one psychodynamic, biological rhythm at our disposition – if only we can learn to recognize it and make use of it: ALTERNANCE.

As a regenerating principle, it has the rare advantages of being simple, free, and capable of helping a majority, rather than only a select minority, of people.

The following facts sketch for us the character of alternance:

- *It is something easy to understand and observe* because it is taking place everywhere, within us and around us.

- *It is difficult to put into practice* because most of society – including the academic world – has been programmed for counter-alternance, towards continuity, rigidly ordered planning, and the rejection of (or fear of) life as oscillating between different polarities. It is because of this that those who wish to start alternating must bring back to life, within themselves, processes that at present lie paralyzed, forgotten, or extinguished.

- *It has become something indispensible in our modern times* since it can free us, without damage, simply and totally, from those rigid, counter-alternant blockages in which we have become joylessly caught up.

By means of concrete examples, this book explains how each one of us can, with a little training and awareness, rediscover alternance – that fundamental pendulum of life without which nothing swings in its natural rhythm.

Alternances in Daily Life

Once the basic idea of alternance has dawned on us and awakened us, we notice that wide-ranging alternances are everywhere:

In Nature

...day and night, stormy and fine weather, daybreak and sunset, still pools and raging seas, level plains and lofty peaks, ruminating cows and hummingbirds...

About the weather: Many people cannot stand the climate in Guadeloupe because from one end of the year to another it stays precisely the same; there is a lack of stimulation through climatic change.

Another example is that of long Nordic nights, almost sunless days with merely a weak glow for a short while; whole months spent in the dark and the cold with, on top of it all, the temptation of alcohol as something which might make the long, obscure winter bearable and provide some stimulation.

In Food

There is a quest these days for "a balanced diet" – always balanced and, effectively, always the same. Therein lies a mistake which ruins health and any possibility of suiting the diet to the individual. It prevents awareness of the extremes which mark any one person's dietary limits and hence the possibilities of their food intake evolving and alternating.

It is not a question of finding the right diet but rather of finding a range of menus, a variety, within which one can alternate, with one thing complementing another. In fact, it will be by alternating between different dietary practices that we will best establish **instinctively** the range of foods which most suit us.

Doctors and wise men of old knew that one should have a really good "pig out" once a month and eat relatively little the rest of the time. Notice how that provided a very basic alternance. Also, consider the once-a-week fast prescribed by many religions as being a very good thing in itself, yet another opportunity to alternate.

One thing is necessary: **to add some muscle to our instinctive feel of things**. By so doing, our research into which forms of nourishment suit us and which enable us to alternate, along with observing our reactions to them – our "body language" – all will contribute towards the development of our instinctive awareness.

Walking

With its motion, now of the left foot, now of the right, the arms swinging in counterpoint, the body twisting slightly from side to side, walking takes us along, allowing us to view frontally and on both sides whatever our life's decor happens to be. It is probably the most balancing physical activity that exists.

This is all the more so since the discovery that on the soles of our feet there is a "map of reflex zones" corresponding to our body's principal organs. This means that walking, especially barefoot on a beach of tiny pebbles, stimulates all of our internal organs.

Furthermore, recently published information from geobiology (the study of subterranean telluric currents) has brought to light a matrix of rectangular links (called the Hartmann network) through which we necessarily move when we walk. This network of currents will evidently have some effect upon us, an alternating influence, since we are continuously breaking through its links and crossover-points.

The Alternating Human Dyad

When two people work together, there occurs not only an addition of their respective qualities but, also, a multiplication of them due to the interaction of their different minds and characters. Co-animation is one example of this and often gives good results. Monks always used to go in pairs; for them it was an essential rule. A single monk was in danger of becoming imbalanced and so was in need of the company of another monk, something of an echo of himself.

Our picture of ourselves develops through human interaction. In the word ''alternance'' itself we have the component ''alter'' meaning ''the other''. For me to exist, there must be you; without you, there is no me.

Harmony, Color, Form and Sound

Here we can evoke the relation between alternance and harmony, recollecting three basic ideas: colour, form, and sound.

- colour relates to the emotional dimension of the person.
- form relates to the will.
- sound relates to thought and consciousness.

It is the interaction of these three elements in the human being which can and does bring about a harmonious and joyous effect. Even the dictionary definition of this word with its Greek origin, *harmonia*, emphasizes the pleasant sensation that is felt.

We readily speak of a harmonious interplay of lights or of colors to conjure up the image of an ensemble which is lively, stimulating and pleasant. Conversely, we might talk of something's ''stultifying form'' to suggest that it is boring and unpleasant, just as the derogatory ''stonefaces'' can evoke the tragic and the unauthentic. In such ways we characterize the difference between the dynamic and the static.

The tolling of a bell, called the tocsin, with its repetitious, monotonous, and prolonged sound tells of death, of danger, of fire or of invasion. Notice that this sound, the antithesis of alternance, is never used to announce something good. On the contrary, however, we have the gay and rumbustious pealing of bells for happy events; what could alternate more than their waterfall of notes? Consider the elemental play between these two and their echo effect.

Biorhythms

We find alternance in biorhythms, too, with these following three parameters:

- increasing energy,
- decreasing energy, and
- energy at the crossover point where it is more or less balanced.

Now here we have a debatable point, for a fixation of balanced energy is a dangerous phantasm. Since effectively all biological balance is, by definition, unstable, something passing in nature, to make a goal, an obsession, of balance can be a harmful mistake. People striving for it will seek, as they often do, something that they will never find, for it does not exist. As a consequence, their lives will be joyless and constantly frustrated.

Diversity in Daily Life

This is the opposite of the standard, the monotonous, and the identical. As soon as nature is no longer held tightly in check or plundered, it manifests a profuse diversity, allowing an infinite variety of possibilities for alternance. So many examples could be given of this.

Alternances are innumerable; the opportunities to alternate, too. But we are not always sufficiently aware of them to be able to put them to use. That is the problem.

The main goal of this book is not to explain alternance but to allow anyone who needs it to make the very best use of it, with all the fantastic possibilities that it can bring about. In order to do that, one needs to regain use of mechanisms which favor alternance. Theoretical understanding alone is of no use; in fact, it is as useless and inadequate as trying to learn to ride a bike solely by reading a treatise about balancing on two-wheels.

The same is true of depression. Everyone can understand that a depression will not be cured simply by reading a medical book explaining its mechanisms. By contrast, however, it has been noticed that depressions are sometimes cured by a sudden initiative or by an external shift in events, or they may be cured by some revolution in a person's inner mechanisms.

This is why, as we have said, this book is composed of some chapters which are explanatory and some which are centered around shifts, currents of ideas and key themes – presenting, without any logic to their order, various elements among which the reader might find just that spark that he or she really needs, the telling image or the situational example, which best shakes the inner springs and cogs and which clicks perfectly with the mood of the moment.

In terms of what we can do about things, all of that comes down, in the end, to two major categories:

- alternances in life in general, which we understand intellectually with our observer consciousness, and
- the alternances of our own lives, the ones in which we are actors and of which we are the instigators. Each of us senses these, hopefully begins to intuit them, and finally enacts them in our own way.

The Alternances in Your Life

Among the innumerable possibilities of alternance which are within you and surround you, on many levels, there are certain to be those which correspond to your needs more than others. Seize hold of the alternances you find in areas of interest which thrill you. Do not try to go beyond your naturally spontaneous areas of interest in order to dryly put into practice some "alternance exercise". That would profit you little. There are so many possibilities for alternating that you will automatically have every chance you need, without going off to seek out the extraordinary.

Whatever the positive shock that this discovery brings may be, or whatever thirst it awakens in you, start off with easy, ordinary things. That will enable you to obtain results which will astonish you without having to immerse yourself in some new method or technique, and without you having to take on board a whole new philosophy.

Minor and Major Alternances

The minor alternances to which one can treat oneself all the time are the most instructive ones and the ones which give the best results.

When your body says "Stop!", that is already an alternance. Sometimes it is not always possible to get up and leave a meeting which is boring you, even though all your body and mind are murmuring, "Go on, go." You let the wish to leave build and strengthen inside until, all of a sudden, you cannot take it any longer. You go. The alternance is all the stronger for it: a great tide.

At night, turning on the light and then switching it off, not really knowing why or, during the day, going first in and then out of a room without really knowing what you intended to do there – this is not just being stupid and brainless. It is often the beginnings of an alternance: our instinct trying to find its way and wanting to wake up. It is not ridiculous and so there is no need to fight it.

One needs to know how to come and go pointlessly; how to seemingly not know what to do or where to go, like the homing pigeon who circles for a while in the sky before finding his direction.

Let these little pointless alternances, these first sketches, reveal themselves: they are the tiny contradictory gasps which are really a beginning of, an instinctive search for, a new way of breathing . . .

You will also think, of course, about **the major alternances for which you have been waiting for a very long time or which have taken so long to become manifest**. These can be the great spring tides, the cleansing waves which change everything, the rush of fresh air through a house that has been closed-up for a long time. Or, on the contrary, it can be the door that one closes because things have been over-exposed to the blasts of the four winds, a closing on whatever has been without any control or disciplined rigor.

For instance:

- Saying to yourself "I'm not going to let just any old thing take place in my life from now on."
- One day to simply close the door on those people you feel to be harmful to yourself.
- To decide to have one fast-day a week, perhaps as taught in the religion of your childhood even though you may no longer practice that religion.
- To quit a questionable professional venture which you can no longer morally go along with and seek something more palatable.
- After having decided not to have children, to become open to the possibility.
- To question the alternance of self-centeredness and altruism in your life.

Why not be self-centered for a week, for example when one is sick? This can be self-centered in the sense of re-centering oneself, like the caterpillar which prepares itself a cocoon before going through the trauma of emerging as a butterfly. One could imagine the caterpillar as being 100% self-centered in devoting all of its energy to itself before the emergence.

This is the case for those who, when they are sick, find it absolutely necessary to defend their lives to the limit: they need to think of themselves, to the depths. It is the case for those who continue to let themselves be vampirized even on their sick-bed where they are at last forced to protect themselves completely. Such a situation can be complex indeed.

Let us be totally self-centered for a certain time and then get out of it, fly away, and do extraordinary things purely out of love for others! What a magnificent alternance!

Do not fling yourself into these major alternances with the pretext of gaining time, catching up with lost time, or getting rid of some vampire or vampirizing situation. All that is very difficult, very delicate.

The major alternances are not to be considered in the same way as their minor counterparts, which can be taken up at absolutely any time to give us a "breather", a break, or diversion. They must and can wait for the right time, their right time. For, you know, it is never too late to open the windows and alternate . . . It is, then, simply a question of know-how and good sense so as not to create violent gusts which could have been avoided.

Alternance has its limits. To want to alternate – at any cost – when one has lost the habit can be sometimes very dangerous.

The Right Time and the Right Means for Living

Sudden and excessive alternance is not recommended. It is like trying to force a rusty old lock; even if the door does open, the hinges, themselves rusty, might collapse. We see this sort of thing with people who take up jogging – the ones you see killing themselves, with efforts of will-power that deny all that is natural, their faces grim and contorted, evidently in a lot of pain. Now the body is very aware and can send you messages if you know how to listen to it. Do not force it into alternances which are too brutal when it instinctively refuses them. A rather interesting book has been published on this subject: *The Wisdom of the Body* by William Cannon.

It is like the fear of serious rheumatism sufferers who become scared that something will break if they are shifted. Movement is something that can only be relearned progressively, and certainly not by sudden displacement. Do you know how painful it is to move a joint that has been in a plaster cast for a long time? That sudden movement is not recommended! It is just as dangerous as using all one's force to thrust open the ancient doors and skylights of a long-abandoned attic, without first carefully lubricating the hinges.

The daily drop of lubricating oil and the first tentative little tremors, the small intention, not yet even a movement but a simple palpitation – this is the key point and already the starting-point. Just that small minimum is enough to start to re-learn alternance, when one has completely lost the habit and the use of it. That is the initial answer and this is good sense.

There are worm-eaten doors, destroyed by non-use, which can no longer be opened without them either breaking or crumbling into dust. However, the human body with its living tissues and organs is not like inert matter, not like latex sap removed from its rubber tree; it can regenerate itself, tissues can be rebuilt, and organs re-enlivened if one knows how to give them the means and the time to do so.

When our minds and our conditioning refuse this regeneration, we know we are really blocked. If that is the case, we need to give things time to settle into place. Then they will proceed naturally.

Alternance – so simple and quite ordinary – is within everyone's reach, since it is everywhere, all around us in the great rhythms of nature and within us, right down to the movements of our breath and those of the heart which beats in a tireless alternance for a whole life.

This book has been written for the majority of people, for those most crippled by "life-shift rheumatics"; for those who have never alternated and never allowed this spontaneous movement; for those imprisoned in the darkness of closed and airless rooms, with worm-eaten doors that they dare not open for fear of seeing them crumble into dust, leaving them without even that for protection.

See then, how you can alternate without breaking any part of those old doors, those ancient locks that you have used to barricade your life. You are not alone in wanting to release yourself from these blocked and barricaded situations, not by any means alone in wanting a robust vitality and a true joy in life; but let us love, too, the gentle process of our awakening and those trembling first steps and give them time.

Some people have a natural sense of alternance as a constant reflex in their lives; others will begin their discovery of it through this book. For others still, it will hopefully start to flourish and be put to better use with the help of this book.

If your health is fine and you are happy, radiantly content, and successful, then you will probably be reading this book for some "fine tuning", or for ways to cope in the future with the inevitable and

normal problems of life. Above all, it might shed some new light
enabling you to understand others better.

If, however, you are not all that happy, not so content, and feel
that your life does need to move forward, does stand in need of a
renewal, and if you somehow feel that alternance could be the right
way of going about that, then please turn these pages . . . one way or
the other.

Emptiness

Each of the three following chapters about emptiness focuses on
situations commonly encountered in daily life:

Fullness and Emptiness is the basic alternance for good health.

Nature Abhors a Vacuum deals with the case of people who let
themselves be invaded by emptiness without realizing it.

Feeling Empty Is Not a State of Mind deals with the case of those
who realize their emptiness and experience terrible anguish because
of it. This anguish can be negative and destructive, or it can be
positive and lead towards a solution.

Fullness and Emptiness: An Unknown Vital Alternance

Life can get overloaded to such a point that one no longer knows what to do next. We can be so "full to the bursting-point" that there is not a spare minute left in our busy daily agenda. This is, more often than not, how it is for "normal" people in our fast-paced society. Even weekends are busy and overloaded; fortunately, in spite of everything, they still constitute a slight alternance through which we can change activities, but they never accomplish the grand and maximum alternance of shifting from fullness to emptiness.

We are unable to achieve this, unable to know how to stay inactive for even a moment, once we get into the habit of being overly busy. One need only observe a waiting-room to see this: most people are busy reading or scribbling. Few are those who stretch, day-dream, yawn, or sleep. At night, too, many people have to resort to a detective story or sleeping-tablet in order to unwind and get to sleep.

Notice here that religions generally incorporate rites or duties which create some alternance between the weekday activities and the weekend. This is the case with the Jewish Sabbath, during which the devout Jew does absolutely nothing, even foregoing the right to make anyone else, whomever that may be, do something. It is also the case with traditional fast-days and fasting. Even though doctors (and "nouvelle cuisine") lay down abundant dietary restrictions, none of them has yet formulated the issue clearly, by stressing the filling/emptying alternance.

It is by no means an easy alternance to put into practice because we have lost certain emptying skills, such as the capacity to soak ourselves in a prevailing atmosphere – in the tonality of a landscape or in the mood of a morning or of a sunset.

Paradoxically, skiing is another way in which we can accomplish emptying. I have often noticed in my medical practice that people manage to somehow cleanse their mind through skiing. They come back from it saying, "The snow has cleansed me".

Actually, that is perhaps not quite the right explanation. The snow-whiteness has something to do with it, of course, but more than anything else it is the fact that, while skiing, one cannot afford to devote even one second of thought to work and worries. If one does, one falls. Skiing obliges everyone, that is everyone but the professional, to be uniquely concerned with their legs and nothing else. More or less the same is true for sailing on a rough sea; one really must be preoccupied only with that. It is a good alternance with respect to daily life.

Reflections such as these allow us to grasp more clearly the lines along which our search for change in life and for a joyful diversity must evolve.

This filling/emptying alternance is not something generally recognized by psychotherapists, who proceed to analyze the emptiness or fullness without appreciating that *one of the simplest things to do is to get the filling/emptying alternance-pump going* so that the empty person fills himself or herself with what is missing and the overly full individuals rid themselves of whatever is too much – and this **without** being overly preoccupied with **analyzing anything whatsoever. Rather than a qualitative evaluation, it is a question of the quantity of things being dealt with**. If alternance can manage to take place, and if it is in sufficient quantity, things are likely to sort themselves out all by themselves.

This alternance is also interesting when applied on a sociological level, providing a key which might partially resolve some of the present social disorders and problems, especially among the young. Some of them have no idea what to do with their time and, to keep themselves busy or to "let off steam", will perform senseless acts of vandalism, or they may steal, perhaps eventually even kill.

Even more than adults, the young have a vital need for activities which can give them a sense of existing, of vibrating, of having done something. This need has been masked or distorted to such a degree that many have come to seriously believe that the gadgets of the consumer society – video games, Walkmans, etc. – are enough to fulfil the lives of the young.

How can we expect our young people to put up with (without neurosis or anti-social reactions) a shrivelled, dampened life of TV images, sensational publicity, and films which, at best, do no more than take their time and their money without giving something back in return, except a feeling of emptiness and non-being.

It may be useful to say one or two words about theft in particular. People often steal to obtain money that they cannot get otherwise, especially in a society unable to provide work for them. However, theft also enables them to vibrate and to do something exceptional in a world which provides little such opportunity, a world in which everything seems possible but nothing is really feasible.

Give the young some possibility of living in a concrete tangible world to which they have direct access, without needing to go through bureaucrats or investigators, then they will be able to express themselves by creating things rather than destroying them. The young break things because it is the only way they have of trying to be a little emptier. **Give them the possibility of employing their vital filling/emptying alternance – both ways.**

We really mean it when we say "both ways"; for to propose that the young, with time on their hands, enter the slavery of consumer society with the prospect of never again escaping is a proposition doomed to failure. They likely have seen their own parents work only so that – in the end and quite openly – the fruits of that labor are thrown on the scrap-heap as broken or outdated waste, and this under the pretext of keeping commerce alive. Many of them refuse now to have anything to do with this. They have no wish at all to be dominated to the bursting-point by a hateful job that overwhelms their life. What they seek, either consciously or not so consciously, is what we all seek, the possibility of joy and the freedom gained in a natural and vibrant alternance.

It is indispensible for the majority of "normal" people who neither steal, vandalize, nor kill to practice the emptying/filling alternance. It enables them to re-establish a balance, release pent-up energies, and earn money.

Three possibilities are open to us:

1. The first way is traditional and straightforward: to allow the practical guidance of our religion to work in our lives, keeping well in mind the fact that we should not try to either water down or modernize certain of its rules, though these may at first appear out-of-date or useless. They can, in fact, assume a new relevance when viewed in the light of alternance, especially their ability in shifting us from filling to emptying and from emptying to filling.

2. A second option is to consider the analogies of science: Science offers a picture of how all of nature's "pumps", including the bellows of our lungs, the pumping of our heart, and the

workings of our intestines, make emptiness and fullness alternate. Remember that pulmonary emphysema is not a sickness of people who cannot **breathe** (as many people think) but a sickness of people who do not know how to **breathe out**, completely emptying their lungs of the air which is dilating the lungs.

3. A third possibility is to heed our intuitions and impulses which, when they are not blocked or deviated, will suggest which beneficial alternances to follow. This assumes being able to let our intuition speak!

We can sum up as follows:

- when you are empty, fill yourself – but not with just any old thing.
- when you are full up, bear it in mind that you should seek opportunities or ways of emptying yourself.

This is sometimes easier said than done.

Some Examples

Early in my medical practice, I adopted two expressions which clearly define two common situations: ''running empty'' and ''running full''.

1. Those who ''run full'' are the workaholics, completely addicted to work to the point where not an instant goes by without something to be done. They never have a free moment. It is effectively very difficult to make them alternate and introduce moments of rest into their pattern of work. It could even be dangerous to blindly insist that they do so. The alternances to which they ought to turn are more subtle than that.

   For these workaholics, their only real rest and their most accessible one is, of course, sleep, provided they are not so exhausted or worked up from the evening's activities that they cannot get to sleep without sleeping-pills. When that is the case, slumber no longer represents such a natural alternance and becomes more a question of sleeping under general anaesthetic. In such circumstances, everything that might help induce a natural spontaneous sleep ought to be systematically tried out:

an after-dinner stroll, a simple infusion, reading a "sleeping-pill novel", etc.

One should not try to stop those who "run full", for it might well induce a depression. This is often the case when life's hazards suddenly deprive people of their jobs or when they find themselves confined to bed with, say, a broken leg. That is one reason why alternance must be sought within their overload of work itself. This is where the idea of skiing, mentioned above, comes in. It is not an idea that is obvious to everyone. When I was a young doctor I had quite some problems with the social services officer who was checking on why I had written medical certificates excusing people from work which read: "2 weeks of rest: skiing recommended."

The problems were soon cleared up when I rang the social services doctor to relate my point of view, giving details of the case, and explaining that if I prescribed the classical fortnight of rest, there would be a high risk of it being followed by three months of depression.

2. Those who "run empty" are the opposite of the above, almost the negative of the photo. Their lives run on little nothings, with which they exhaust themselves, more or less aware that their activity, going around and around in circles, is of little use and leads nowhere. Some are avid collectors of pointless objects, pernickety souls who fill their lives with extraordinary meticulousness centered on the worthless. They often pass through periods of "unexplainable" exhaustion. Although it is difficult to help them change their attitude through traditional psychotherapy techniques, things can become gradually more acceptable by getting them to introduce small alternances into their lives.

I remember one collector who was rich enough not to have to work for a living. He was often ill and did not realize that his life was just going around in circles. I suggested that he play a more active role in his collectors' club, not only be an ordinary dilettante member but to take on some responsibility, lend more help, and contribute his opinions to their work. In doing so, he discovered his skills in organizing and this led him to look after liaisons with other groups and clubs. Alternance, between his collecting and other activities, was now happening all the time. His life became more panoramic and oxygenated, and his illnesses disappeared.

I also remember quite a few people who in the post-World War II period told me, "Doctor, I'll tell you something in confidence and it's this: I was cured by the declaration of war! It's true – from that day on and throughout the fighting I had no problem and no sickness. It's pretty astounding but that's the way it's been."

Comment: What is war if not an uninterrupted sequence of some periods which are full, where everything builds up – to the point sometimes of total submersion – and some periods which are empty, in which nothing happens or one is waiting. Ironically, those alternances can bring a measure of health back into balance for certain people, those who previously may have been overly wrapped up in themselves or stuffily boxed in by monotonous activity.

Nature Abhors a Vacuum

In the earlier days of my medical career, I was like most young doctors in wanting to drive out sickness and to "re-educate" people, to rid them of their "faults" and mistakes, so that they would no longer get sick. Although I already knew illness to be the consequence of accumulated error, I had yet to realize that removing a mistake or fault without taking care to replace it with something else is, in itself, an error.

Now I understand everything to be long-winded, more intractable, complex, and enduring than is easily dealt with by illuminating fault, accompanied by a good telling off, or cured by some corrective gymnastic or by goodness-knows-what miraculous remedy.

That is why, for a long time now, I have instinctively developed the habit, either in the seminars I lead or in the medical consultations I give, of bothering less with people's faults and failings. Instead of putting all the emphasis on reinforcing and boosting whatever qualities they have, I work to enable them to make the most of their personal ingenuity.

Every Individual Has Their Personal and Special Ingenuity. This ingenuity is something to be discovered and if it is not immediately obvious then pains must be taken to find it, for it is certainly there. Neither the therapist nor the patient should feel satisfied until this ingenuity has been discovered, fortified, and amplified. Why? Because only it can fill the place left vacant by the relinquishment of error and failing.

I use the well-known, evocative, and here quite appropriate expression "nature abhors a vacuum" to sum up this general situation.

A general application of this physics notion is also to be found in microbiology, in situations where one wants, at all costs, to destroy or drive out "a bad microbe"; for there is a risk that as soon as that particular microbe has been destroyed, another and sometimes more virulent one will appear to take its place. In such a context, we can appreciate the utility of techniques that aim at re-introducing "good microbes" into an organism and not merely at destroying the bad ones.

We can see that grasses and greenery will invade wastelands everywhere. Even the tiny cracks of a concrete sidewalk will soon be taken over by vegetation, lichens, and mosses. We readily observe this law at work in the external world but rarely apply it to ourselves. And yet . . .

Some people lead such full lives – so full that nothing more can be slipped into their busy timetables. In their case the absence of vacuum is particularly obvious.

Curiously, those whose lives are "empty" are singularly ingenious at filling the void with useless things. Try and take away one of these illusory details and you will see their reaction: they clutch onto them like a cat clutching the branch of a tree while below is a ferociously barking dog. The great psychoanalyst Ferenczi even noticed that some women who longed with all their heart to have a child but who were unable to become pregnant ended up by filling their stomachs with intestinal worms. Moreover, I observed this phenomenon myself in the days when anti-parasite treatments were less efficient than they are now.

Another significant fact is that when someone is really empty and not even to able to fill his life's emptiness with those "trivia which become everything", he will manage to fill it by creating a neurosis. He may be invaded by a terrible fear, a neurotic anticipation of something that does not happen.

Psychological treatments which claim to analyze the causes for such a vacuum, in order to remedy it at its source, are often doomed to failure. They can worsen, sometimes considerably, the cases of those who undergo them because they try to replace the vacuum with an analytical accumulation of that which provoked the problem.

Then the psychologist, or those close, say, "He needs something to occupy his mind." This is, in fact, to some extent true for it is obvious that these "emptied" people will feel much better once they have some activity which preoccupies them and from which they have no possibility of escape. Its constraints, the obligation to work, are what sometimes can put the life back into them.

Once she has had a child, or several, a mother is overwhelmed by a host of difficulties; she has something to worry about every moment. A really good difficulty, a gnawing worry, holds its own without question. It is sometimes said: "One worry drives away another", implying that we have been designed to work to the full – not empty!

But here notice that the expression, "the joys of family life", has double meaning:

- the straightforward joys emanating from a happy, invigorating, family life and
- the ironic use: to refer to the deluge of problems that this saying can evoke.

Whichever of these two "joys" apply, they can create volume, effectively filling time and space.

Emptiness, as a sickness, cannot be filled as simply as turning on the appropriate tap and filling a container because here we have closed vessels, refusing anything which might replenish them. Walking proof of this are those who feel forsaken and forlorn even in the midst of a crowd, finding no one who "really interests them": that or those for whom they are longing are always elsewhere, inaccessible, or with someone else.

It is in those cases that the mechanisms and potentials of alternance can be of most help, for alternance provides a basic technique, a common denominator. The idea is not to find a distraction, some ideal activity which would fill the space, but to **alternate**, because a succession of small unpretentious alternances can quite easily weave some fabric into this void, filling it infinitely better than just one unique ingenious occupation which, as soon as it is over, will again give way to an awful feeling of emptiness.

Once they gain the spontaneous tendency of following their intuition and thus of getting out of their neurosis, they will start to create a whole succession of minor daily alternating tasks.

These tasks will comprise minor household duties: phone calls to see how this or that person is getting on, or to wish them happy birthday, or to remind them of things planned together. They might go out to buy a newspaper, check up on some concrete task and set up its different stages, deal with a friend who may need help several times a week, etc.

The particular example of rich ladies busying themselves with worthy causes, having a schedule overrun by myriads of things to be done which require their presence, is a case in point. To whatever degree they have sporting activities or have a niece or nephew to worry about and for whom they have to do something very concrete, and in all the ways they "give of themselves", their life is woven with alternances, often keeping them in good physical and mental shape.

Nothing Makes Us Alternate Any More – Whereas Everything Made Our Grandparents Alternate. One chief characteristic of our modern age is the creation of free time, either in terms of vacations or due to the array of machines that now deal with the daily chores which took up most of our ancestors' time. We have cars, telephones, washing-machines, dishwashers, various express services, etc.

We no longer realize it but our material lives have been unburdened quite fantastically. Inasmuch as life used to be weighted down with material difficulties, today this unburdening could hardly be more of a hollow gain for certain people.

Liberated by the systems and services now at their disposal, people rush to stuff their life with the stupidities, the hype and the gadgets that the consumer society has created for them. Typical of this are organized vacations, from which they are likely to return, more often than not, disappointed; such a structured vacation has saved them from having to, as the telling popular expression goes, "kill time". Even honeymoons are organized these days and have become a familiar catalog item.

These are the people who have not yet the common sense to find the right sorts of rhythms and activities for themselves. What they need is to grasp the fact that a varied program, an alternating one in fact, is what will help them to make the best of things.

From every direction we hear praise for the merits of continuity, the wave-free, one-track efficient life. Everything encourages us in it. It is remarkable when one realizes that, with respect to the idea of alternance, monotony is a form of continuity.

Alternance brings a corrective factor into our lives, in the form of rediscovered menus of alternance that must often be worked out and tailor-made for our lives. This corrective element has now become a very urgent necessity. Some obvious alternances would be, for example, to jog if one has a sedentary life, or to go and to see a horror film as a change from the noiseless, padded life that the present conditioning of humanity affords us.

One very striking instance is that of passionate love, which seems able to replace everything else in life and which, at first, leads one to say, "I am filled to overflowing". The classic unfolding of this situation is that one then wishes to preserve that fullness (the word is charged with meaning) and so one gets married. But this fullness can dwindle so easily with the passage of time; everything tends to shrivel up, to crumble, and so then one may decide to have children – the next traditional step. Children become "the joys of family life" mentioned above.

Too often these days, that is still not enough, and so the next step may be divorce, one of the current reasons for which is "we have nothing left to say to each other". This is one way of formulating the idea of a vacuum and contrasting it with the fullness.

We can conclude from the above that, in the evolution of our present world which has taken the direction of continuity and standardization, **every time that we have a choice** between one way, which is **continuous** with what went before, and another which is an **alternant, let us develop the reflex of choosing, at least as a possibility, an alternance rather than continuity**.

The fabric of life which will emerge from this will always be of better quality, with little possibility of emptiness enduring between its tightly-knit, well-woven knots.

A Relevant Example

A man comes into my office, closely followed by his wife who was obviously worried. He must have been a fine figure of a man in his younger days. His medical record says: "68, professor, retired, stomach ulcers, depressive by nature."

He had been, in fact, a very well-known university professor as well as writer. I learn that his health had been fine until he retired. He had fallen ill several months after his last book had been published.

I immediately and intuitively felt the inner drama taking place in the life of this famous figure with respect to reaching retirement. I asked him what he was doing and what his plans were. His wife did the replying for him, explaining that the first thing he must do was take care to look after his health. He added that he had no plans and that his life had come down to following his diet and taking lots of rest.

As far as I was concerned, there was little doubt about the diagnosis: this important figure had become "emptied" and, as "nature abhors a vacuum", he was now filled with sickness. Calculating the shock it would deal him, I suddenly said, "Leave the ulcers to me – I'll take care of them. Now, let's talk about your future.'' At the word ''future'' he was taken aback.

I continued, ''Sir, you are one of the great men of our times, a specialist in your profession, known throughout the world. You cannot keep to yourself all those things which you know but have not yet published.''

I sensed that I had hit the right spot. The man, a little stooped and with eyes that spoke only of sickness, suddenly straightened himself and the flash of a certain brightness – a flash that I have come to recognize – fleeted through his look. I knew we had won.

Following this, it took me a while to reassure his wife and explain that he should not work more than his body allowed. I would give him a prescription that would help put back the missing physical strength and see him in the very near future to check that all was proceeding well.

It was a different man who left my office: a man already filled with his new future. He set himself back in balance by oscillating between writing his books and the relative vacuum of his retirement. His medical treatment posed no further problems.

Feeling Empty Is Not a State of Mind

Emptiness, on a human and biological level, is probably one of the least known of phenomena and, in any case, one of the least understood and most under-evaluated among our various psychological processes.

It seems paradoxical to talk about an "empty" life in these times of over-abundance, when the majority of people complain that their lives are full to the bursting-point, complaining that they no longer know what to do next. They are so overloaded by things to be done, people to meet, facts and objects to deal with, all of which keep them super-busy but often without anything of note being achieved.

We will see that this is not paradoxical at all and that, moreover, **it is probably the monumental error of our age to consider as full that which is, in reality, tragically empty**.

I was first taken by this idea of the omnipresence of emptiness while observing some young people – restless, apathetic-looking, idle, and immersed in the noise coming from their constantly worn Walkmans.

As a doctor I had for a long time noticed a terrible emptiness overshadowing some people in certain quite comfortable circumstances. Those close to them were unable to understand it at all, astonished that "someone with so much at their disposal" could feel in the least bit empty; to them it seemed that these rich people, so bored amid their opulence, were nothing but "ungrateful so-and-sos".

Rare it is for the poor to feel empty in their difficult lives, for they are in need of everything. Even though some live in what can be a pitiful destitution, their lives are never empty.

What's Going On?

The feeling of emptiness is, in fact, "psychological", a state of mind
that one gets into. Now someone else might come along and tap the
person who feels empty on the shoulder and tell them: "Hey, you
have no reason at all to feel so empty. Your life is totally full – just
look at how you live, surrounded by all these conveniences and this
abundance of marvelous things!"

There is a lack of understanding between these two: between the
person who experiences and complains about emptiness and the
person who would really like to have in their own life "all those things
that Mr. Empty has". This common situation has struck me many
times during the course of my medical career.

**What element, then, can a doctor, and more particularly a
psychologist or psychoanalyst, bring into this situation?**

They can at least contribute understanding and an ear. They
know, through their experience, that the person who feels empty is
really suffering and *really* empty – even if the emptiness is purely
psychological and just "an idea they have gotten into".

It Is Here That This Book's Suggestions Come Into Play. This emptiness
has been more or less considered by many doctors and
psychoanalysts in the past as being a state of mind, an attitude that
one needs to just drive out, a bit like driving out flies. These days,
however, it ought to be considered as a physical and biological
reality, of the same order as a stomach-cramp when the stomach is
empty or, the contrary and very painful case of the same order, as an
abscess bloated with pus that one wants to have removed, even
though this is not always possible.

- One can be filled with emptiness or
- filled with pus – with "harms" that one wants to get rid of but
  cannot, whether through lack or strength or skill.

A fresh look needs to be taken at:

- on the one hand, "emptiness" and,
- on the other hand, "that which is full of harms". These, in fact,
  encompass the same problems.

By looking at these two with new eyes, we can gain a clear
perception of this phenomenon of emptiness, which is generally not
at all a "state of mind" but a physical and biological reality. Once

emptiness has been rightly defined and well-measured as a concrete reality, and not as something psychological and abstract, then we can go on to discover how to "fill up its vacuum".

Abstract explanations can only increase the vacuum and the uneasy feeling it creates. Therein lies a serious mistake made by the psychology of recent decades – that of speaking in abstractions to people who are literally dying of an emptiness which has replaced the concrete fullness of life.

What is needed, then, is to lead them into tangible, living situations, to sources of action and into taking decisions; above all, one must avoid making the mistake of emptying without filling. There too, classical psychoanalysis was mistaken in spending its time tidying things up without replacing them with something else.

And this without remembering that **nature abhors a vacuum**.

Noise and Silence

Noise and silence are two clearly perceptible opposites between which we are able to alternate. That seems plain enough, yet the young, and now a growing number of adults too, are quite happy to trot around with a Walkman on their ears. What is the nature of this phenomenon?

Adults often demand silence in order to be able to express themselves, to focus and concentrate themselves, or to simply just get away from noise. For them, one of the charms of the countryside is that there they can manage to find their silence – in the woods, in their reflections, and in sleep. Concerning the latter, the particular sensitivity of some people to noise (which upsets them or stops them sleeping) can make their neighborhood a terrible problem for them, their rest being disturbed by the slightest barking of a dog, or the resounding clickety-click of the upstairs lady's heels on an uncarpeted floor at midnight.

In the countryside, the cock crows without disturbing anyone. However, it must be said that the sense of space there is very different, people are not stacked one on top of another. In town, legislation prohibits farm animals and often car-horns too. Noise can be, in contemporary society, a constant preoccupation.

A somewhat unintentional experiment in Sweden, on the noise/silence relationship, remains famous. It took place in a major automobile company. In the name of social progress, they had decided to do away with the partitioned offices which separated people from each other and to put everyone in the same vast, modern, and attractive space. The concept of landscaped offices was born.

In order for people to be able to work well and discuss things properly in such a space, the designers were asked to incorporate efficient soundproofing into the system, so that the cacophony and indiscretion that might occur due to the proximity of these office-cells did not become nuisance enough to damn their whole project. The architects summoned the most famous experts in soundproofing.

The results were surprising and created widespread interest. On the first day that the system was put into use, one could have heard a pin drop in that work-hive of juxtaposed offices hyper-rigged-out with noise-traps and anti-echo baffles. The eerie silence generated so much anguish that the designers had to urgently send someone to a railway-station or some other dreadfully noisy place to record sounds. These could then be fed over loudspeakers, in the right dose, into this bureaucratic universe which they had so successfully drained of all noise and impregnated with an unnatural silence.

What are the norms for noise and silence? Only after examining that notion can one possibly talk of alternance.

At this point one can bring in the current controversy between some adults, parents perhaps, and the majority of youngsters. "Anti-Walkman" adults wonder how the young can live in the middle of such incessant noise when what these adults hear, be it called noise or music, seems to them to be, on the whole, unbearable for "normal" ears.

How things stand at present is that this (for some deafening) noise of rock music is hardly heard any more in public; except, say, when the proud purchaser of a brand new "ghetto-blaster" turns it on as he leaves the stereo store.

Sometimes this music is literally deafening: Many young people, drunk on the joy of being continuously plugged-into their favorite music and constantly imbibing its pulsing rhythms, do become, medically speaking, partially deaf, registering below-normal thresholds on audiograms.

As a doctor, concerned with understanding the equilibria at play and with grasping what is happening biologically, I have of course questioned all this myself. I had a curious and chance experience. Wondering why I had not looked at television for so long, I had decided to watch it a bit and see what was going on. I installed myself before the set with this marvelous little gadget that enables one to change programmes by remote-control from the armchair, and proceeded to switch channels, just according to whim. I spent the whole afternoon and part of the evening and night doing this. I was dumbfounded and flabbergasted.

Emptiness.

They fill us with emptiness.

Working from there, and my television day, I returned my attention to present-day advertising, so tremendously sophisticated and thought-out, to the point where it has become a science: the science of intrusion into the personality; the science of persuasion directed at and against all defences. It is all quite unhealthy and can lead to distinct disorders of the psyche.

Seen in that light, the Walkman, and its incessant music, becomes an ever-present, always available means of saturation. One no longer needs to defend oneself against advertising; it is unable to intrude (or intrudes much less) because the space is already occupied.

In terms of volume, the young are immersed in ''a system working at a level of constant saturation'' and this probably preserves their balance in this world of advertising, filled as it is with hollow and tragically empty things and working from no other reference-point than the constant preoccupation with selling.

This saturation selling has reached such proportions that it has become normal to say that one needs to know how to sell oneself, or that a politician did not know how to market his image and so was not elected. Common folk in France had pre-empted this new approach, now apparently a necessity in election campaigns: They used to say, long ago, when listening to a political address, ''There he goes, selling his salad'' (*il vend sa salade*).

Some are deeply preoccupied with maintaining, for a little while longer, this consumer mentality, a mentality that a growing number of other people are rejecting but which no one knows how to modify without the whole consumer society disintegrating in the process. There is the bad, the less bad, and the good – for yes, there is good in society but how to discern it? Where is it and what are its limits?

Hence, the sound immersion in which our young feel happy probably does contribute to their staying balanced in this world pervaded, as it is, by false statements, sham, and artifice; where the key to joy is never freely given them, except perhaps by their parents who themselves may be over-burdened, intruded-upon, and who themselves may be insufficiently protected by their own inner sound level. When too low in relation to the outer background noise, this inner sound level can be overwhelmed and ignored.

How then, can one conveniently establish desirable alternances between noise and silence? Apart from places of meditation and retreat which one visits for their very special form of silence, we must recognize here the difficulty of setting down a general rule. It is up to each individual to find their own norms and particular forms of alternance.

To see the young, or not so young, on the street, obviously invaded by the music of their Walkman, is not necessarily to see someone surrounded by noise. It may be, on the contrary, someone having a moment of alternance, getting away from the tom-tom of the social background-noise by creating their own zone of counter-noise. It may be the only way available to them for gaining access to a form of silence or, at any case, for creating a barrier against being filled by just any old thing.

Noise/silence is, of course, a very necessary alternance. However, as we have just seen, it is likely to be choked in paradoxical disguises which we must try to comprehend and interpret in the context of new sound levels within our society.

"The Green Thumb"

Trees and plants can provide us with a great deal more than the soothing charm of a show of greenery. They are veritable gifts of nature, able to put strength back into us, sometimes within minutes, by simply being with them. One needs to know that this is possible and one should really consider making use of that possibility.

We would like to go a little further than just mentioning the above potential and, in the few pages of this chapter, we will deal with the subject of plants in terms of the numerous and rejuvenating alternances that either those in our homes or the ones that we cultivate can provide. This is why we have pivoted the chapter around the "green thumb" phenomenon, familiar to gardeners but unknown to many. This is a pity because those most in need could obtain stimulations from the plant world which might well compensate for the manifest imbalance of their lives. Another aspect is that we are all living these days in surroundings invaded by various sorts of new radiations about which we are relatively uninformed and unaware.

In Moments of Great Fatigue: Trees

Once, when discussing the support that trees can provide when one is emotionally down or physically tired, one of my friends who today at 85 continues to live a very active life, reminded me that some fifteen years before he had been suffering from severe exhaustion. I had advised him to go to a forest and place himself against a tree, picking one he found especially nice and feeling it to be the right one with which to enter into contact. The result was instantaneous. In less than ten minutes he was re-charged and felt a lot better. Since then, he has passed the "trick" onto others and continues to use it himself from time to time.

The Technique of Getting Recharged by Trees

It is one of my medical prescriptions. Not for everyone, of course; some people would never understand. One must take individual sensitivity and bias into account.

Someone who is exhausted and wants to try this technique should follow their intuition, not their reason. There is no particular category of tree which is beneficial and the main thing in choosing a tree to enter into contact with is to choose it using "love". In our particular region the oak is often the ideal tree. The kings of France dealt out justice beneath oaks and the oak played a key role, as well, in Druid ritual. The oak leaf ornaments certain military caps to denote grade. In brief, if you like the oak, use it: you will not be the first. You can face the tree and take it in your arms or you can turn your back to it and rest your spine against its trunk.

If you do face the tree and place your arms around it, make sure to have a magnifying glass or some entomological instrument in your pocket. If someone suddenly appears while you are embracing the tree, you can quickly take out your glass and pretend to be observing an insect deep in the bark. It is important not to seem crazy in the eyes of those who have no understanding at all of this sort of thing.

You could equally well take a walk in the forest and absorb the ambient energy and beauty, while looking at the sky through the high branches. Once you have made a habit of this, you will have acquired the possibility of recharging yourself from trees.

"God's Tree"

Once when speaking of how much trees can be of help to those in difficulty – trees, with their roots deep in the earth, their tops in the sky, and their leaves and branches captivating energy – the person I was talking with suddenly shivered. Showing me the goosepimples on her forearm to prove her surprise, she said:

"Strange that you should mention that when we barely know each other and could have spoken of thousands of other things. Your 'tree' story struck a chord in me on account of my brother who is a missionary, a priest in the Far East. He works in a leprosy center run by five nuns; he says mass every morning for the sisters there. He cannot communicate with anyone; they all only speak the Bengali dialect and he can't understand a word.

"When he arrived at this desolate semi-desert, full of suffering and almost at the end of the world, the only thing which immediately struck him was a tree. The tree, like him, was alone. It had been planted at the end of the missionary garden. He told himself straightaway that that tree would be his friend and would help him to live there.

"So, every day, he would go and visit his tree and it is from the tree that he draws part of the strength that enables him to keep going in that desolate place. 'One would believe,' he says, 'that the Good Lord put the tree there too, all alone.' "

Not everyone can have the spontaneous contact that this priest had with his tree at the end of the world. But who of us, reader or author, would be willing or able to assume his life to experience this? On the other hand, he has no need to learn how to reanimate his alternance reflex because his life is constantly oscillating, we can imagine, between a heaven so high and an earth so harsh.

We can, however, take a small step in that direction by keeping house-plants that we have to take care of ourselves. Maybe you already belong to that coterie of gardeners who love and care for plants, those who swop information about plants that you cannot find in books. They will tell you:

"Now don't put a tiny shoot in too big a pot – it will feel lonely and wilt."

"Talk to your plants – they will grow the better for it."

"Don't leave those two plants together, they don't get on well and might harm each other."

"Pick a clear sunny location for these plants and a shady one for those over there. Watch your plants' reactions in order to sense which spot suits them best."

"I often see you sitting in that corner where you used to have plants but you took them away because they were always dying there. Better be a bit careful – that spot might be harmful for you too."

"Let him prune your trees. Even though he has never had a course, he knows, has a feeling for it; he sees what is to be done. He has a green thumb."

These common themes, often heard among those who have an affinity for plants, may be quite surprising for the uninitiated who might well feel more like laughing than sensing a new well-spring of original information, potentially of use to themselves or to others not gifted with that type of extra-sensory perception.

Now that you have been made aware of the phenomenon, you who do not have a "green thumb" can tell yourselves that whenever you come across someone who does have one you can profit from their sensitivity to the vegetable world. Rather than scorning those with this gift, let them help you.

This might help you to no longer just mechanically buy yet another houseplant, the one before having wilted and died without you even wondering why. Some of the things that one learns in these areas are extremely useful, helping you avoid spending too much time in places that are not good for you, places that you may find "unsettling" or "tiring". You might become more aware of vague comments you make about places and the feeling they give you.

You might be inspired to change the location of your desk or your bed. If the change has been for the better, then you won't have to feel that you are becoming superstitious: you will be able to formulate explanations based on another possible way of perceiving the interaction between living things.

Do not be afraid of developing this "sixth sense".

But How Does This "Green Thumb" Phenomenon Relate to Alternance?

The point is that whenever you are looking after either the plants in your home or the flowers, vegetables, or trees in your garden and try to perceive them "instinctively", you change worlds; you bring into play, among other things, the right side of the brain which has become relatively atrophied by the overwhelming rationalism of our society.

Rational left brain/non-rational right brain: a basic alternance.

"When I get home from school," a teacher once told me, "I like to spend some time looking after my plants. It makes a change of world."

To be able to "change worlds", passing from one side of our brain to the other (its opposite in some ways), just by caring for plants – what a beautiful opportunity if one is willing to seize it!

Plants: Developing a Sixth Sense

House plants represent a very convenient way of developing a green thumb because anyone can have them. Every time you take care of your plants with a wish to "understand" them, speaking to them if needs be, you well and truly quit your rational being to **physically** make contact with your nonrational being in an area which poses no problem or danger for your personal balance of mind. It is **without danger, convenient, and inexpensive**.

Let us stress again this word "physically". What is going on here has nothing to do with reason, forced imagination, simple or complex techniques of meditation destined to seek out the abyss-like depths of the subconscious: it has nothing to do with a course or an initiation philosophy. It is this: a physical, concrete, and straightforward contact.

Further, it is without any danger. So many techniques claim this yet, in reality, do create side effects, negative weakenings of certain aspects of the personality. So much so that this particular way of enhancing oneself, really and truly without danger, should be seen as an opportunity to be seized and given very special attention.

It is difficult, once we have decided to develop one or another facet of our personality or of our individual potential (notably in the area of extra-sensory perception), to find freely-given exercises that are danger-free, given the publicity, weirdness, dangers, sources of imbalance, and swindles that one finds everywhere. There is considerable risk of falling into aberration or exaggeration: no longer knowing the border-line between, on the one hand, that which is naturally balancing, instinctively extra-sensory, and useful and, on the other hand, that which is likely to lead to madness (i.e., loss of control over one's own judgment and loss of correct evaluation of the boundary between the crazy and the reasonable).

A discreet and alternating play between the rational and nonrational is automatically triggered every time you nurture your plants in a certain state of mind and with a certain degree of attention. This can stretch us beyond the habitual and limited materialism into which we are often plunged.

Apart from their beneficial radiation which is studied more and more these days, plants can thus provide us with an opportunity of making repeated forays into "the other territory", the other shore of our personality, our non-rationality, our extra sensory perception, and our intuitive feel for the less-obvious, hidden, balances. This, in turn, is one way of progressively and safely reconstituting an ensemble of perceptions that society, over time, has lost, to the point where just the inkling that those things might lie dormant within us, ready to be awakened one day only now begins to appear.

The Helpful Influence of Animals

Edward Twitchell Hall's book *The Hidden Dimension* studies the unique space which marks our personal territory, our body-field; within this space it is difficult for us to tolerate any physical intrusion. The configuration of this space varies according to race, culture, and circumstance but it is always there to either protect us or trouble us without, for all that, being something visible or generally acknowledged.

Why is it that lion-tamers and tiger-tamers always stay beyond certain very precise limits when handling the big cats which perform for them? It is because they have come to well understand the question of each animal's minimum personal perimeter. They know intrusion into that space will directly threaten the animal and could provoke an attack.

There are hidden dimensions and influence-relationships between people and things around them that we do not see directly but nevertheless sense from time to time. With a little bit of help, these things become much clearer and directly perceptible.

Animals can often be revealers of things which we ourselves perceive poorly or not at all. Dogs are obvious examples of this, with their powerful sense of smell and constantly alert minds, keeping a look-out and sleeping with only one eye shut (as seen in cartoons). These are qualities no human possesses. Use of dogs for protection or hunting goes back into the distant past. Man has used animals as an amplifier of his own perceptions for a very long time indeed: the inscription CC (*Cave Canem* – Beware of the Dog) on the pediments of rich patricians' villas in ancient Rome bears witness to this. Maybe it concealed a reality even more complex than that of just the guard-dog that we think of today.

Another example is that of the geese of the Capitol saving Rome by their extraordinary vigilance. (See note below.) Maybe they too had another role of which we are quite unaware. In the Far East, studies have been made of certain animals which "foretell" earthquakes. Our ancestors, too, took a lot of pains to observe plant and animal reactions in order to work out their weather forecasts.

Note: Sacred geese were kept on the Capitoline Hill of Rome. When the Gauls invaded they sent a silent contingent up the hill, but the geese began to cackle, awakening the Roman garrison.

Today we keep animals more for pleasure; as a remedy for boredom or because they are handsome, intelligent, or valorous companions – so serve our dogs, cats, and horses or the swans which beautify the lakes of country houses and parks. Rarely do we have them as real witnesses of our lives, and this is a pity for they have much to offer.

It is possible, even probable, that certain animals played this broader role in past civilizations: we recall here the cat that was deified, for example, in Ancient Egypt. Paintings and objects that we treasure as remnants of former times give us ample testimony of this. In the present day, animals play a fringe role in our society, apart from those owned by farmers, or by hunters who love and appreciate their dogs, or those kept by animal lovers, say, a writer who observes a pet cat's behavior from close quarters and who may simply like to have the "very special and helpful presence" of its company. Most people do not take seriously the fact that animals could contribute something positive and alive to a daily routine that may have become sterile, synthetic, insensitive, and lethal for our dynamism and our developing extra-sensory perception and intuition.

From a physical point of view it is obviously beneficial for some people, retired or sedentary persons for example, to have to take their dogs for walks. Everyone realizes that. That is the first alternance that the animal brings us because whatever the weather, no matter how lazy we feel that day (or perhaps we are in that state of torpor brought on by central heating and TV), whether flopped out on the couch and with rotten weather outside, Bonzo has to be taken for his walk. And what a splendid good it does us!

Animals, dogs in particular, can incessantly offer us opportunities to alternate, depending upon the variety of their own activities. "That makes me think of my mother," a friend once exclaimed. "She used to say her dog drove her mad yet, for all that, thanks to the dog's presence she was much happier and more dynamic."

We all have encountered examples of that sort of thing. Let us call them **minor alternances**.

How are we to interpret the strange "extra sensory facts" that we sometimes witness with disbelief or astonishment: the behavior of animals who occasionally understand more about what is going on than we ourselves do and who try to help or protect us? They show, at times, a remarkably instinctive flair for discovering what is best for us. We might have heard of, or perhaps have witnessed, incidents where a cat settles down on precisely the spot where someone has trouble (the liver, the stomach) and brings them some relief. Or stories about dogs where, from the day the master falls ill, the faithful companion never leaves his master's side, takes care no longer to jump onto his bed, stops barking (unless it is to warn others of something gone amiss), and who generally gives a much appreciated help through constancy and a reassuring presence.

Their awareness of psychic pain, of "grief", seems to be a commonly accepted fact. They feel when you are down or depressed and come to comfort you. It could be that the help they provide is not merely psychological but also of a magnetic order, recharging you, in some way or another, from the natural vitality which surrounds them.

I remember a friend, a lady, who was very moved by the death of someone close. The downstairs neighbor's cat came up to visit her and then quite definitely settled itself in for two months, bringing her a certain comfort. The way it helped had nothing at all to do with the sort of help humans give. It belonged to a different order of things and took place on another level: it was an alternance.

Where all this becomes much more interesting is when there are major alternances, bringing the deeper mechanisms within us into play.

Have you ever watched a group of young children or even a single child, still at an age where spontaneity has not yet been stifled by education, watching a beetle moving through a tuft of grass? When the children (or the child) have a choice between the tuft of grass and the "playground" (invented by adults to keep children busy), they will rarely opt for the playground. In the playground they do not alternate, or if they do it is very little. But with the beetle in the tuft of grass, they are in another world, without dimensions or limits: the world of wonder.

This small example is sufficient to point out that knowing how to enter into the world of animals can be enough to set off a whole series of chain reactions and help us change realities. What follows is an anecdote showing the wealth of knowledge that can be had by observing animals.

Domino and Bloudy: A Therapeutic Dog–Cat Conflict

It took place during the summer holidays. Domino, a 3-year old black fox terrier, unimaginably spoiled, was accompanying his mistress, a member of a group working collectively on the publication of a scientific book. The foundation's headquarters, the location for their joint effort, was set in gardens and had apartments and various facilities and through all this roamed a 2-year old cat named Bloudy. Bloudy had his little ways, his habits, and his circuits over which he reigned as absolute master in his peaceful and bone idle existence.

When cat and dog eventually came face to face, armed conflict had to be avoided, as it often must among civilized people. There was regression to the stage of armed peace (or "peaceful co-existence" – whichever you like) with each of them being held back on a leash or kept separate from each other through complicated rituals of doors and windows.

Then came the period of "detente", the "thaw in relations", with each being able to pass near the other quite freely, without doors or barriers, yet nevertheless maintaining, deep within himself (visibly) a powerfully-rooted hatred of the other – or, at the very least, the thought that he could inflict a healthy thrashing on the other were it not for the obligatory detente.

Thus passed the summer, with brief episodes of wild pursuit when tempers spilled over, episodes we immediately cut short as the local peace-keeping force. The summer and the work on our little group's book came to its end. Each of us returned home to again enjoy his or her personal territory, quiet at last, sheltered from the intrusions or abhorred presence of others.

It was a peaceful autumn, then winter, the time when everything slows down, even wars, the time when it is good to stay at home, eat and sleep, far from the cold's aggression.

It is the time when those who have pets dread their putting on weight and try to avoid the portliness caused by good eating, long naps, and lack of outdoor exercise.

They knew what this normally meant for Domino: he tended to become like a fat sausage and so needed to be pitilessly rationed. This kept him on the lookout for possible sources of food all day and put him in feverish anticipation of meal times. For Bloudy, things were not so clear cut, being younger and in less risk of pudginess. Besides this, he was a cat and extra weight often shows less on cats, who tend to stay feline and are not so easily fattened-up.

In the autumn we noticed what turned out to be the first surprising consequence of Domino's summer: everyone who had not seen him since before the summer holidays and who were not aware of all the adventures and psychological tribulations he had undergone, found him much thinner, elegant of course, but also quite **rejuvenated**, having acquired a dynamism, a spontaneity that he had previously lost in his "spoilt bachelor" days. One should note the fact that everyone expressed the same idea: "younger-looking" or "rejuvenated", rather curious and unusual terms to apply to an animal.

To be absolutely truthful, one should also add that he went through a sort of depression on his very first days back home, before rediscovering his lost youth. For a while he was flopped out in an armchair, sad, and uninterested in his food. It was the trough of the wave.

The second obvious consequence was to be seen during the following winter. Despite long hours on the sofa and the perpetual quest for extra food whenever the occasion presented itself, he had much less tendency to put on weight.

The dog, Domino, kept his psychological gains. With a certain maturity, a keen eye, and glossy coat he was more on the alert for possible feline competition than ever, always watching the cats on the street below with an air of dominance, punctuated from time to time by furious barking from his fifth-floor balcony. His sense of social hierarchy had definitely made some progress. From being a dog with no experience of the world's diversity, he was becoming a creature more and more capable of handling complex situations and maintaining his position.

In the family circle it had always been the habit at Christmas to distribute presents at the time of the main feast. Everyone got something, including the pets. Domino, now confident due to the progress he had made, took not only his own toy but also a few that were not destined for him, doing so with new authority. At the same time he was getting into a new game of surveillance, sensing and testing the limitation of other animals' territories. It was very much like the homecoming of voyagers and old soldiers who, on their return, exercise a natural leadership and authority which somehow seems due them because of their wealth of experience. And so, as was evident to all, Domino was a dog reborn through his trials and conflicts with Bloudy the cat.

This story would only be of anecdotal interest for animal lovers, were it not for its medical implications which are instructive and indicative of the more positive outcomes of a conflict situation. We were amused to observe this confrontation between dog and cat, but the mechanisms set into motion in our psyches had nothing to do with those that would have been brought into play were it a conflict between humans. It was and is a different world. To be able to witness those mechanisms was for us, without us knowing it, a vivifying and instructive alternance.

Having to learn to decipher the attitudes of an animal, to understand what is going on it its head, and to foresee its reactions sharpened our powers of observation. Animals cannot speak. One has to guess and that obliges one to become more sensitive. To keep on switching from human society to animal society is an opportunity for major alternance.

Whether they be witnesses to our lives, or actors within it, animals can be an inexhaustible source of observation and information. They can be astonishing mediators, teaching us to better understand and perceive certain types of relationships we have with our environment. It is just this rapport that society or an agitated, artificial life may screen from us.

To live in a balanced way, full of bounce, with a dog or a cat in the house, or maybe even chickens, a cock and geese in the yard, with a cherry tree and some apple trees, is perhaps a formula to be rediscovered.

Managing Your Time Differently

Other than a tendency we had as kids (and perhaps still do, in moments, as adults) to "let off steam" – which is a form of alternance, if not the best – nothing has truly taught us to alternate . . .

When we were children we got our fingers rapped and were told: "Stop fidgeting like that, shifting from one foot to another, you're making my head spin! Do your homework and stop dawdling." Thus has our alternance instinct been battered, yet in spite of the abuse, it still remains alive.

Once we became adults, we were obliged to repress our fundamental alternance to such an extent that the only way it managed to come out was when we let off steam. Sexual repression, which some psychoanalysts still place at the center of various disorders, is nothing these days (in our opinion) when we compare it with the more general repression of the movement of **our inner pendulum**, our time-manager.

All it asks is to swing, to beat, to alternate – as our heart beats, as our breathing alternates, as day and night, and almost every natural phenomenon does.

Our Abusively Systematic Education Helps To Get It Stuck in Continuity. "Don't be unstable, follow-up your idea, stay with it, stick to your agenda" is what one hears all day long. Schedules, programs one after another – the sickness has even infected youth. Fun is no longer allowed to just happen but it must be self-controlled, methodical, never scattered, and must fit in with the whole.

Natural diversity is taking place everywhere around us and it can act as our guide, provided that the pendulum of our alternance has not got stuck. If it is stuck, then the thing to do is to free it. This is possible.

Fortunately, most living things are nearly always reparable. Even though they may be crushed, rigidified, and stultified by years of anti-natural, non-ecological practices, our life forces usually ask no more than that they be allowed again to function and to breathe – as soon as we give them the chance by easing the grip by which they have been artificially bound. They are like the tufts of grass which manage to grow even through concrete. Such is the case for our alternance pendulum, which years of continuity and being stuck in formal logic have probably not managed to completely destroy.

How can one get this tremendous and spontaneous oscillation energy going again, flowing effortlessly and joyously, weaving automatically in life, as regular as our heartbeat or the working of our lungs, without us having to think about it or making any effort? This is a question which we try to answer in different ways in this book.

Once the movement of your internal alternance pendulum has been re-established, you will notice that you make different use of time and timing; that, for example, your subconscious is able to develop a new and astounding "flair". Two sorts of example relate to this. The first is one that we have all experienced at one time or another, without even noticing it; in these moments we have reanimated our pendulum without knowing that was what we were doing.

Many people have noticed that they frequently come across the idea or information they are after, not when they are at their desk with a blank sheet of paper before them but when they have nothing at hand to write with, for example, in the car. It is at those times that the most brilliant ideas and crystal-clear intuitions seem to emerge.

Then comes the thought "Right! I'll keep a tape-recorder in the car from now on to instantly collect and preserve these brain waves." Generally, however, once the tape-recorder is going, the inspiration dries up. In any case, nothing is quite as good as it was: the thinking is heavier, more explanatory, more reasoned out.

What happened? Driving a car brings about a change of activity, another environment, away from the office or desk. The world through the windshield is full of ever-changing images but, unlike a movie, other real people are there – and traffic, difficulties, "hiccoughs", and the unforeseen. It is in the middle of this hotch-potch that brilliant new ideas and rare intuitions arise.

Once the tape-machine is installed, poised to record, there is no longer a real alternance, for the car has become a mere extension of the office. The rare idea no longer blossoms.

The same thing happens with skiing. All those who practice the sport know that one has to think uniquely about the skis, otherwise one falls. Ideas often crop up on the slopes, when one is wrapped-up and bemittened, without a pen.

Some well-off people conclude, by observing this, that the mountain air and the snow are inspiring for them. They have a chalet built in their favorite spot. Strange to say, once the chalet is built, the spot may stop being so propitious: no more ideas, no more real relaxation like before. They look back with fondness to what was previously discomfort, the unexpected, and change. Yet another fact is to be reckoned with: the more comfortable the chalet, the less likely are creative ideas to pop up. The time has come to lend the chalet to friends!

The second type of example refers to the extraordinary meetings we may have at some odd bend in a path. "Pure coincidence", cry the experts in statistics and probabilities, "that sort of thing just happens from time to time." What they do not take into account is the curious fact that these chance encounters more often than not occur in places where we ought not to have been and on paths that we ought not "normally" to have taken.

The same applies to objects that turn up at the least-expected moment – except in one case that I remember well. It concerned a lady relative of mine who believed in God and who practiced her own form of religion, thronged with saints, each endowed with a speciality, a little like the gods of old. Whenever she had lost something, she would say "Oh dear St. Anthony, please make me find this object." And quite regularly she did find it.

One way to see this, without in any way disparaging the interplay of spiritual realities in our lives, is that St. Anthony may have acted like an alternance reflex. Having searched methodically for the lost object, she then changed register completely, shifting over to a more instinctive feel for things, to a secret way into the pockets and folds of her memory inaccessible to her conscious mind. Then it would click. She could find the object, a needle in a haystack if need be.

Some people who follow initiation paths, and others who have undergone certain trials, will sometimes confide that they have a sort of "gift of second sight" or a sensitivity which enables them to find ways where others only see barriers blocking the path. They will also tell you that, through whatever meditation, prayer, or spiritual method they particularly use, they have acquired an extraordinary sense of intuition which they would never previously have thought themselves capable of.

Instead of simply admiring them because of this, or nurturing a blind wish to be just the same (which often leads to aping them without having understood anything in depth), we can begin to interpret what they are telling us in the light of the alternance concept.

Instead of trying to copy what can never be copied – the inner psyche of someone else – you can instead begin to see in what they are telling you an example of the possible results obtainable by animating alternance in your personality and setting the fundamental pendulum of your life back into swing.

Some Relevant Examples

Let us consider the example of the life led by Benedictine monks. Knowing their day to be an uninterrupted sequence of oscillations between the cultivation and preparation of food, manual work, mental work, and ritual, we see here that the alternance-pendulum is part and parcel of their everyday life. The example they have been setting for centuries in this domain is, when one thinks deeply about it, quite phenomenal.

The use of alternance in joyful living could progressively become just as evident in our own lives if we bring into them the same element of variety the Benedictines have. You could consider introducing some physical activities to complement your mental ones and your meditation (or whichever form of self-transcendence through prayer you prefer). The inverse also applies: you might add the spiritual dimension to that which tends to be solely physical or material. The important thing is to make sure that the whole picture is an alternating one.

One of my patients once went through a crisis involving an intuitive revelation concerning the meaning of life. The crisis was of such proportion and so intense that he would normally have had to be placed in a psychiatric hospital as someone temporarily insane and needing ''to be led back to reason''. I do not take sole credit in saying that it was only due to a quite exceptional and in-depth medical understanding of the case by those caring for him (in terms of the evolutionary value of what was happening to him) and the help of his exceptional wife that the man avoided hospitalization.

The crisis lasted for eight days; in that time the patient rode a gigantic and continuous wave of intuition which made him switch never-endingly from one activity to another, alternating day and night, following the pendulum swings in astounding fashion:

- He would start eating.
- After two mouthfuls, he thought he would be better off in his underwear out in the sun. He got undressed.
- He went back to the food but then immediately got into the idea that it would better to do a little gymnastics. He broke off eating again.
- Having barely started the gymnastics, the next thing that came with some insistence into his mind was the thought that it would be even better for him to pray and thank the Lord for his meal. Etc.

Viewed from the outside, all this was obviously crazy. The astonishing aspect which drew the attention of the medical staff, who were exceptionally competent, was the fact that the patient had acquired, simultaneously with his hyper-activity, an unmistakable gift of clairvoyance, a faculty that he had never had before. Thus, every time the phone rang, he would know before his wife picked up the receiver exactly who was calling and what they were going to say. A similar thing happened with the radio: as he turned the dial, he described in advance the discourse that was taking place right then in Parliament.

Much more significant than the above events was the fact that, by having gone through all those rapid alternances, he did manage to get himself back into balance. Besides this, the amount of physical and mental tidying-up that he accomplished, in both his house and his life, was tremendous, frightening almost.

Once out of his crisis, the patient became once again swept up in a wave of duties emanating from the social continuum. This effectively shut off any possibility of alternance dictated solely by intuition and fancy. He rapidly lost his power of clairvoyance but he had nevertheless gained some ongoing benefit from his crisis in the form of an appreciable heightening of his intuition and, we should add, in the discovery of alternance's tremendous potential. He has maintained these to this day, that is to say, for some twenty years.

Although the above is a very unusual example, it gives us a magnified view of how alternance is often linked to intuition.

"It's not so unusual as all that," explained Peter Roche de Coppens when he read the above paragraph. "It's exactly what happened to me a few years back, except that in my case it only lasted a few hours and not eight days.

"At the time when this unusual experience took place, I was

exhausted, stressed, and depleted due to a long lecture tour and the prolonged, intense work needed to finish two chapters of a book – not to mention university problems. I started that particular morning with an ardent session of prayer and meditation. It doubtlessly sparked off the things which subsequently happened. Anyone witnessing these events would probably have taken me for someone suffering from hyper-activity or simply as someone unbalanced.

"I had barely started my first lecture of the day when an inner force, a compelling thrust, made me get up from my chair, write on the blackboard, walk abnormally around the lecture hall, sit down, get up again, etc. It even got to the point where I left the room twice – the first time to go, unnecessarily, to the bathroom and the second time to make a phone call which could well have waited.

"The lecture over, I went home and it was there that it occurred: what I have since learnt to recognize as a series of alternances taking place at an ever-increasing rhythm and apparently without reason. First I listened to some of my favorite music – but very briefly. Suddenly, I got up and called my secretary at the university, saying, 'Um, hi! I just felt like hearing the sound of your voice.' Then I sat down to read a James Clavell novel. Next I went to write a letter. Following this I started reading-up for some research I was involved in. Unable to stick with it, I went off for a stroll but, barely past the threshold, I decided to go back in and do some gymnastics. Then I started cooking food. Having eaten my lunch, I took a siesta and fell into a very deep sleep.

"I woke up three-quarters of an hour later, completely renewed, relaxed, and recharged. I was myself again, feeling quite calm and 'normal'. I got back into my usual rhythm of activities, remembering the incident as merely a bizarre crisis that had done me a lot of good.

"It is quite apparent, Jacques Pezé told me, that the series of rapid alternances I went through acted as a radical, but extremely simple and efficient, remedy which probably occurred to compensate for too large a stretch of time spent in a continuum and too long spent living on my nerves and will-power. Proof of its beneficial effect lay in the fact that the exhaustion and constant feeling of stress, that had been with me for days on end, disappeared immediately and that I emerged from my siesta in terrific shape, ready and renewed for action.

"On the grounds of my experience, I would advise anyone who undergoes an adventure similar to my own, with these particular sorts of rapidly-alternating impulses which do not go as far as to make you a crazy person but simply get you very activated, to offer yourself the little luxury of simply following the alternances. It will probably do you a lot of good and give you some direct experience and understanding of the very alternance mechanisms which are being suggested in this book.''

Such were Peter Roche de Coppens' reminiscences and comments on this matter.

Without going as far as the events in these cases, which are, it must be admitted, exceptions, I can assure you, for I have witnessed it hundreds of times, that each time that:

You feel: *tired* or

obsessed or

insomniac or

more *furious* than is reasonable or

depressed, with time dragging on and on, or

impatient wishing everything to happen more quickly and hoping for things ''to be finished before they are even begun –''

Then if you set yourself alternating (i.e., employ your ''pendulum'' so that it uses time differently) *all will change, almost immediately.*

Practically:

• your exhaustion will diminish or disappear completely,

• your insomnia will no longer be unbearable (no more restless shifting from side to side in your bed – instead you will be doing something else)

• your anger will become diluted by whatever other activity it is that you have switched into,

• your depression will be alleviated by the other things you are now doing and

• your impatience will become the capacity of waiting for things to happen in their own time – meanwhile your alternative activities will be keeping you busy.

So there you have the secret of the whole thing: a very simple secret that is easier to talk about and understand intellectually than to put into practice. However, as soon as you do manage to put it into practice, everything will take place just as I have told you and just as I have so often observed in my patients. Give it a try. Do it automatically and without looking for complications. Then it will produce results.

Every time that I have had my patients do it (often even by phone) there has always been a result: they have started managing their time differently.

Making Changes Is Easier Than You Think . . .

"The course of action I am about to launch into, the objective circumstances now entering or leaving my life, the decision I have just taken: is it all merely a change or is it a real alternance which somehow will make me shift from one shore to the other?" Once we have discovered the importance of alternance and its dynamic possibilities, these are the kind of questions likely to come up at some point or another, in hopes of getting a clearer view of what is going on.

Some people pursue change because they find it a critical necessity for their own self-renewal. However, if they only knew how to make use of the host of alternances that are already at their doorstep, they would be able to satisfy their need for renewal in a much deeper way.

On the other hand there are people who dread change, finding it disturbing and worrying; nevertheless even they nurture deep within themselves a secret wish for change, as something which might relieve their routine. They, too, could benefit from the alternances surrounding them, which need not cause the upheavals they dread.

It is, furthermore, very useful to know how to spot false changes: the ones which tire our health, over-excite our nervous system, and ruin our wallet for zero result. Changes which are likely to be later thrown into question. In brief, it is advisable to see clearly what is change and what is alternance.

Changes are part and parcel of life. We are all the time changing clothes, our glasses, say, or for women, perhaps their hairstyle or make-up, etc. It can go further: change of apartment, of job, perhaps of partner . . .

In this, we are aware of two contradictory feelings:

- *attraction to what is new* because it is the thing which is going to bring some improvement – well, at least, be different – already a point in its favor.

- *fear of what is new* because it might be catastrophic in terms of the way it affects the habits we have acquired, the things we had before or knew before and which held no surprises. Maybe it will be a trompe l'oeil that will end up leaving us frustrated, irritated, and impoverished.

We are so often torn, hesitant, worried – sometimes even paralyzed or imbalanced by the interplay of these two. One observes two main dispositions among people:

- those who find the new so stimulating that they are prepared to risk abandoning the past they have known, relegating it to the deepest dungeon without a second thought.
- those who are so anxious about the future and the bad surprises it might hold in store that they prefer to block off any possibility of change and instead anchor themselves to habit, to well-trodden paths, the reliable, the time-tested, and the stable.

Generally-speaking, people find change easier and more attractive when they are younger, perhaps because they have the feeling that all life is before them to put right any mistake. Maybe too they have not had enough experience of error. To criticize the young because they want change too much or the old because they do not want it enough may be to ignore this consideration.

Whether we are predisposed for or against change, one has to recognize its necessity, on account of its attraction and rejuvenating quality. Even when we reject it, through fear of it, it remains as a pole of attraction. We might wonder why.

Humans have a profound need of progress. However, the only way we progress, radically, is to pass from one situation, one habit, to another. This is very readily observed by turning to the past and looking at all those turning-points, historical events, discoveries, changes or alternances (we will see the difference between these two), and perhaps even difficulties which have become the milestones of our development.

Let Us Now Try To Situate Alternance with Respect To Change. From a theoretical point of view, if we reason using an "If . . . , then . . . " relationship – much loved by mathematicians and computer wizards – and we look into the reciprocity of these two concepts, we observe that *alternance necessarily implies change* (even if one does not perceive it taking place) but *change does not necessarily imply alternance*.

Example of reciprocity/non-reciprocity:

> *If it rains then I take an umbrella. The converse (reciprocal) is false because if I take my umbrella it will not necessarily rain.*

Same example with alternance:

> *I have back pain and so I change mattress. In general the back pain continues.*
>
> *I have back pain and so I sleep on the floor. The back pain disappears.*

In the first case there was change (without alternance): I shifted from **soft** comfort to **soft** comfort. In the second case there was an alternance (and, of necessity, change because there is a change involved with every alternance): I shifted from **soft** comfort to **hard** comfort.

We can see from this that since every alternance contains a change, then the simplest thing to do would be to always look for alternances rather than just changes. That way we are sure of getting, at one and the same time, the effect of alternance's good influence on our health as well as the effect of change's novelty.

Theory and reason, however, are often far removed from real life. Where things become a little more complicated is when certain alternances fail to give us the feeling of change. Even the idea that there is, in fact, some change may not occur to us; this is while the alternances (continually taking place – for example, breathing) could be permanently furnishing us with an inexhaustible supply of change – changes which are marvelous, always renewable, free, not dependent upon our efforts (thus leaving us more freedom). So natural and basic are such changes that they can breathe life into the very roots of our existence – if only we knew how to make use of it.

Perhaps the most typical example, because it is the most commonplace, is breathing. Breathing is a process so automatic that few even think about it. Who would ever consider it as a possible source of any sort of pleasure or, more than that, as a change? And yet . . .

Certain facts give us clues about possible lines of action. A considerable amount of yoga has to do with breathing, not so much as an oxygen-pumping process but in terms of its movements, its significance, and its relationship with our different bodily "envelopes," our "higher" bodies. Apart from yoga, breathing only catches our attention when we cough, when we lack air, or when we have some respiratory infection. Only at those times does breathing assume its true value.

There are other unnoticed, unused alternances:

- day/night, sleep/waking state – these are alternances which, without consciously noticing them, we live through all the time, for better or worse depending upon whether or not we know how to simply accept each for what it is and swim with the wave as it rises and falls.
- sun/rain, wind/stillness, humidity/dryness – which we do not experience as changes but as ''caprices'' of the weather, to which we are subjected.

All these alternances, which are in fact radical changes, are not lived as changes. To pass from night to day or from storm to calm feels much less like a change than, say, buying a new tie or a new shade of nail-polish. That is the reason why it is so important to situate alternance correctly with respect to change: to do it in a way which draws the maximum from each situation while, at the same time, avoiding traps.

Alternance can comprise a large change when, for example, one goes from the heat of the Arabian desert to the intense cold of the North Pole or it can be a small change when, for instance, one goes out of a heated room into the chill fresh air or, even more simply, if one just opens the window to ''freshen things up a bit''.

In biological terms, the principal difference between change and alternance is that one can live without change (by locking onto the habits of the past) but one cannot live without alternance, without occasionally at least ''opening the window for some fresh air''.

The person who accepts alternance or who stimulates it when it is seized up or insufficient lives carried by the waves which are the master rhythms of life. The person who refuses it lives in a watertight coffer in the middle of a sea which is at times agitated, at times glassy. Exhausted by trying to keep the box still, even when the sea is calm, he does not realize how much better off he would be climbing out on top of the box to make the best of the fine weather. As for times of storm, everyone knows that it is better to run with the waves than to try to oppose them.

We measure all these differences and sometimes do instinctively respond when we feel weighted down and look for a diversion to relieve us from a tiring situation which seems to drag on and on.

Let us take an example. I am at my desk, studying a technical book. Suddenly, I have had enough. My eyes and hands seek out something to bring a change of idea – ah, a newspaper! I go through the headlines without really reading them. They teach me nothing but then, do I really feel like learning anything at that particular moment anyway? What I really feel like doing is relaxing, airing my mind a bit. All those technical, serious, professional chapters have drained me of life. The ''Foreign News'' page brings me a whiff of fresh air from the outside but it is still not enough. It is merely a change. In the end, I pick up a novel that had remained on the desk for some time. With that, at least, I take myself for a moment into another world: the world of imagination. That is an alternance.

The trap there would have been to have given way to the easiest solution and turned on the TV. Then I would have stayed limply in an armchair stuffing myself with images.

By reading the technical book, I was filling myself with others' ideas – a flow was coming into me (input). With the TV there would be a similar direction of flow entering into me, invading me (new input). Although there is a change in the nature of the incoming data, and even the incoming mode, there is no alternance. I have no possibility of expression. I needed in some way to get something out of myself (output) in order to alternate and counterbalance the deluge of data from others.

An even better solution would be to go out into the garden for a moment. Ah, pity! It's raining. Maybe I should face up to the rain. That would, in all events, be an excellent alternance for relaxing me. Another solution, often found instinctively, is to telephone a friend. Then I would really exit from my own situation and enter into someone else's domain.

It is a commonplace, classical, situation in many people's lives, though varying from individual to individual, this search for a way of unwinding, some break, a little alternance. There is a whole range of possibilities.

Sometimes alternance constitutes a radical change and is truly felt as such. For example:

- when we decide to stop lazing around on a holiday and get back into some work or, equally well, we decide to stop killing ourselves with work and take a rest.
- when we opt to live in the countryside and work in town.

The above are experienced as alternances because they are

provoked and conscious alternances occurring amid the innumerable natural, unconscious, or automatic ones which are keeping us alive and which are the fabric of our ''life breath''.

Conversely, numerous changes – as changes alone – are attempts to find something different in life but such attempts overlook the need for alternance. They do not become part of the tremendous coming-and-going movement, weaving our time fabric and continually regenerating us. For example:

- changing the colour of the wall-to-wall carpeting in the living room. It still remains, though, ''a carpeted living room''. The alternance would be to do away with wall-to-wall carpeting altogether, or maybe even to not have a living room any more!

- another funny example comes in the words of a well-known writer who, speaking about one of his friends who spent his time changing wives, said, ''All those wives – by each of them having to be different they end up all the same!''

It is a neurosis to constantly chase after something that one never gets, or that is never satisfying, or that always requires yet another change even though the last one is barely over. We each have cases of this readily at hand to observe.

To renew ourselves then, rather than running after changes which are often difficult to bring about and frequently burdensome, the simplest and most efficient thing to do is to make use of the profusion of alternances which are available to us. But before we can make use of them we have to learn to recognize them. To start with, there is a miracle which is renewed every day, and this is waking up after our night and taking a breath on the threshold of the new day; it offers itself to us in total freshness, absolutely new, if we can but learn to leave the weight of yesterday behind us in the night.

The Beneficial Alternances

By developing new orientations, we will then be able to use ''beneficial alternances'' to satisfy our need for change. We will discover, in these beneficial alternances, what are in fact marvelous changes. They are simple, profound, and infinitely renewable. Some examples would be:

- a cloudburst – the heavy rain which brings some people immediate relief from the tension built up by the coming (dry) storm. Notice that it is asthmatics who appreciate this sort of change for its true worth.

- the rays of the setting sun which, each day, change the colours of your home or apartment . . .

Keep working at it until you discover vivifying changes occurring in what are just run-of-the-mill alternances. Things that normally go unnoticed because they are so natural: the cycle of the four seasons, for instance, which allows living things to recuperate in the winter, then to emerge fresh and regenerated in the spring. It is a question of how aware one is of such rhythms.

We can discover that every evening when we go to bed we participate in a tremendous change that takes place, every day, every night. In the morning we wake up to a brand-new day. Each day is a fresh new day – with, of course, its routines and maybe even its monotonies. However, one needs to be open to the changes which might and could take place and, besides that, to be open to the ones that are already there, taking place but unseen, for every new day is an alternance which adds new fibers to the fabric woven by the past. When we actually live in such a spirit, a whole new approach to joyful living has begun to take shape.

Something can emerge this morning, after the alternance of the night: a risen being at the gates of dawn, standing at the threshold of a day to be lived. To set out into a day which is just beginning, without the burden of yesterday, breathing again – what splendor! Given the banalities in which we are all more or less immersed, even if you miss this overture, day after day, because you jump out of bed straight into yesterday's rut, every day, every morning, the possibility will again be reoffered to you.

Here, it is not a question of suggesting that you become gripped by some sort of obsessive observation, scrutinizing every minute of your life to discover what invisible and magic things it holds. It is simply a question of awakening, for example, this "morning reflex", through which you tell yourself, "I've woken up, after this night when I could have gone to sleep once and for all or where I might have been suddenly attacked by goodness-knows-what illness and here I am, up and about." It is the sort of miracle that we generally only appreciate when we are emerging from a severe illness or a car accident.

"Up, at the start of a day, still yet to be built and shaped. Of course, much is already predetermined by my duties, timetables, and appointments but still, most of that is waiting to be done by my own hands. And, too, there will be something more to discover.''

The day/night, night/day alternance is that: to know how to start out from zero every morning with a totally fresh day before us. Fundamental change, free of charge, is given us through the day/night alternance and through the possibilities offered us by the unknown day ahead – in any case, partly unknown. This is a possibility offered us whether we feel it as such or not, depending upon our ability to modulate our life with time. The great pity is that there are times when we realize that we have been unable to be aware of these possibilities. They were free, they were in the palm of my hand, and all I needed to do was to close them in my grasp.

Alternance and Change: Recognizing the Difference

Change is often difficult, costly, and painful. It gets worn out and always requires more change.

Alternance demands nothing. It is very forgiving, pardoning all to those who know there will always be, as long as there is a tomorrow morning, an occasion to seize joy. It can be automatic, spontaneous, and not tiring at all, once we know how to swim with the wave. By training ourselves to it, we acquire a whole new way of ''breathing life''.

Even if you are running around in circles, endlessly changing the curtains and carpets of your life, the knowing wink of the new morning will always be there, even if you are not aware of it, ready and waiting for the day when you do, finally, take notice.

Relevant Examples

One of my patients, whose life could be described with the term used earlier as ''empty'', was always trying to fill it with changes. While her husband was away on trips, she would have all the furniture in the house shifted around. Each time he returned home, he found nothing in its usual place. As far as he was concerned, the alternance was nil, for he was confronted with the same inconvenience at every homecoming – shifted furniture!

Once, when his wife was away for a week visiting her sister, he had the whole house repainted, instructing the workmen not to paint behind the furniture. His wife, after her return and as soon as the husband was off again on a journey, set about her usual shift-around of the family furniture. The result was frightful, since the changes exposed the previous colour on the unpainted sections of the wall.

These people were very rich. The next time that the husband was away, the wife, in a fit of rage, had the whole house repainted but this time, of course, included the patches of wall behind the furniture. Then she could continue the rearrangements that her husband loathed.

These continued to the point that, during one of his wife's vacations, he decided to bring in some railroad workers and have them bolt down each piece of furniture with those gigantic bolts which secure railroad sleepers. Each item was now attached in a way almost impossible to take apart!

I was just a young doctor at the time, lacking both the weight and the experience to insist upon the solution to their problem: the practice of real alternance rather than their unalternating changes. It was a real need for this unfortunate and too-rich wife. Also, besides being too young, I had yet myself to discover the virtues of alternance.

Breaking Through Blocks in Therapy

It was by chance (well, not quite, but you know how these things are!) that, during the years 1968–70, I first managed, along with the mathematician Professor Arnold Kaufmann, to put my finger on alternance as being a basic key for solving a considerable number of human problems, whether social, economic, or political but also, clearly and simply, individual ailments.

By applying alternance to psychoanalysis, one obtains a new understanding of its mechanisms and this enables us to appreciate them in a new light – perhaps even to rethink much of psychoanalytical therapy. The way this works is illustrated by several examples here and will be treated more thoroughly in another book, *Psychoanalysis, Psychotherapy and Alternance*.

In order to practice psychoanalysis, it is necessary for one to undergo analysis oneself. Towards the end of my own psycho-analysis, when things were dragging on a bit and I was wondering whether or not I should stop it there, whether it was now over (although psychoanalysis is never really over), suddenly I was "cured": I found the solution, just like that, through alternance. This happened during a trip to the United States, which obliged me to switch from the standards of French society to those of New York.

There I met Moréno, the inventor of psychodrama, who was living and practicing psychotherapy in an American context. The shock was quite something – a major alternance. This is how it happened. I had interviewed Professor Moréno for a newspaper. As I was getting ready to thank him for his time and leave, he suddenly said to me, "And what about you young man?" I told him that I was just coming to the end of my own analysis but that neither my analyst nor myself were sure if it was really completed.

Moréno looked at me for a moment and said, "My dear fellow,

you have so much imagination that you'll need a whole century of psychoanalysis!''

·Amazed, I responded, ''What should I do then?''

He looked at me again, drew close and, slapping me hard on the shoulder, said, ''You have to live, my boy!''

I was confounded. It was brilliant: I ought to stop asking myself questions and act. I had just met with a genius. All of a sudden, everything had become simpler and directly accessible.

Thus, and in just several minutes, I sorted out, clearly and so obviously, almost physically, the psychoanalytical problem in which I could have been stuck for a long time had I not, quite simply, alternated. At that time, I didn't know that this was the very best thing I could have done.

A few years later, still not aware that I was practicing alternance, I managed to improve the condition of, and sometimes cure, a growing number of patients coming to see me with unsolved, or seemingly insoluble, psychiatric problems. Some of them had also been going through interminable psychoanalysis. I cured them by steering them to something else – always something other than that which they were living through. That was my ''thing''. I gradually came to be more and more clearly aware of this. Although the ''thing'' changed every time, it always kept the same root – alternance.

This carried on until the day circumstances led me to initiate an alternance, even though I was still unaware that that was what I was doing. This particular alternance was completely unalloyed, involving, from my end, neither psychoanalysis nor a strong projection directed at me as psychotherapist, neither reaction nor non-reaction on my part. In this particular case, the only thing I did was to stir up the alternance process from the outside – without knowing the inner content of the situation. Here are the facts as they appeared to me.

I had recommended that one of my friends, whom I knew too personally to treat myself, see another psychoanalyst. One day she phoned me to say that things were going very badly and that she really had to consult me professionally. She turned up, thin, quite out of sorts, worsened by her psychoanalysis, and no longer sure which saint to pray to next. To see her in such a state worried me a great deal, as did the fact that it was I who had steered her, with every good intention, into psychoanalysis. In brief, I plunged into the situation and we started to talk about her case, her analysis, her sexual problems, frustrations, impulses and repulses. It took a good hour.

Then, all of a sudden, I had an idea, a common-sense reflex, and switched the focus of conversation, from artificial, over-sophisticated talk of role-transfer and counter-transfer to a direct discussion about her as a woman and the psychoanalyst as a man. At times she had deliberately turned up to see him in super-light summer clothes. This led us quickly to the fact that she fancied this chap and that deep down she wanted to discover what sort of person he was without his white coat. However, on account of the psychoanalytical barriers and gibberish, she had never told him this clearly and would never be in a position to do so, because everything was being processed through codes and theories.

Then I brought a new angle into play to extricate her from this mess. Knowing her to be quite tightfisted, I suddenly asked her how much time and money all this had cost her over the last two years. She worked it out and it was obviously quite a shock. Then I asked, "Why don't you just tell him the naked truth of the situation next time you see him?" That is, that over and above the common ground of psychiatric therapy he turned her on and that it had, in the end, cost her dearly to be able to come round, after two years, to saying so, clearly, intelligently, and straightforwardly.

She carried out the suggestion. The analyst proved incapable of absorbing the shock and again tried to carry their dialogue into the psychological labyrinth where he was the game-master. She, however, was still savoring the bitter taste of her spent thousands. Besides this, she had just had a psychological exchange with me in clear, uncomplicated terms and was determined to press forward and no longer play around. She had literally crashed into her therapist (in the psychological sense, of course) and he was unable to extricate himself.

The situation had been demystified and inversed, almost to the point where the patient started-up the analysis of her own therapist. It was a total alternance and its result was near-miraculous: the psychoanalytical treatment, which had dead-ended, was now severed. Things had crystallized in her mind through other means and the analysis, now of no use, terminated itself of its own accord, quite naturally.

In so doing, it was clearly alternance and the kind of change that it is that had once again played the key role: change of language, of rhythm, of scale of evolution, of attitude in analysis, and the change of passing from being the pupil reciting her lessons to being a grown-up no longer needing to recite. What really took place was not just change but alternance – transition from one thing to its opposite, like the passage from night to day or hot to cold. That is what alternance is: change through oscillation; one leaps right to the opposite, to the other side of the line and back again.

A Psychoanalysis Blocked by Lack of Alternance

One of my patients used the following words to describe her situation: "With my first analyst, I strived for a year, trying to get him to say something. With the second analyst, I had to strive for two more years to get two words in, myself. Now I'm here, because I've been told that you do things differently from all that."

This woman was full of wit, intelligent, wanting to sort herself out, and capable of rapid progress in the resolution of her problems. In fact, all she asked was not to get blocked in a system of continuity. She already had a charged social life which demanded continuity from her. She was not coming to a psychotherapist to find even more rules and regulations which would, effectively, amputate the possibility of her expressing herself to the full.

Successful Psychoanalysis Using Alternance

In effect, most of the cures I have obtained in psychotherapy have been based upon alternance, in particular by alternating between verbal expression (during consultation) and written expression (at any time outside of the consultations); also by changing the rhythm of consultation and even by turning around the roles, with myself getting down on the psychoanalyst's couch and playing the part of the client by way of demonstrating the method.

Use of constant oscillation between verbal and written expression came to me quite naturally, as that was the way in which I myself had undergone analysis (under one of Jung's collaborators). The use, when appropriate, of personal-situation-switch, where I became psychoanalyzed by the patient, was something explained to me by an American analyst. As a man approaching the end of his career, he had a wealth of experience and was able to relate with great lucidity the types of cases in which such a role-change had been possible and fruitful. It goes without saying that this particular method is never employed when there would be the risk of further unbalancing a patient too fragile or too young to be able to work through it in a way that, for others, could bring out flexibility of perspective and a maximum personal teaching.

Out of the Rut of Either/Or: Introversion/Extroversion

These two labels are of little help: "You're an extrovert."

"You're an introvert."

Even though they are classical diagnoses made by many psychiatrists, they are incomplete – false almost – because they steer one in a wrong direction. In the light of alternance, we can say:

"Your alternance pendulum is stuck in an extrovert mode."

or

"Your alternance pendulum is stuck in an introvert mode."

This sort of diagnosis is effectively much better because it already contains some notion of, and points us towards, the direction which the actual therapy should take: as a corrective aimed at re-establishing the intake-output rhythm. This comprises:

- **intakes and outputs, well-proportioned in their quantities,**
- **healthy rhythms of exchange-mechanisms**, and
- on a more general level, **sufficient outputs and counter-actions** or reactions emerging from the inner world, the "personality", when faced with pressure and intrusion from the outer world. This is needed to the extent that those who know the person will automatically say, "Well, she is one who doesn't put up with any old thing; she reacts."

Classically, one says that introverts are centered upon themselves. That is wrong: they are rigidified within themselves, frozen in a fixed posture with respect to intrusion; this is due to their inability to produce some counter-pressure in reply, some cleansing exhalation, some form of expulsion which would purely and simply cast out whatever had penetrated them (like coughing when one has inhaled some toxic dust). Introverts stiffen through their inability to react.

Various forms of reaction to intrusion from the outside world can be noted:

- *expulsion*: one coughs, one spits and it's over, as we have just seen. This expulsion of foreign bodies (when one has the strength to "cough") is what happens when people get angry and break things. They "get it out of their system."

- *exhalation*: one exhales a by-product or piece of information which has already been of use in one's life, just as one expels air full of carbon dioxide that will be re-cycled by plants. Not rejection but **participation in the vital exchange-mechanisms of the external world**. This means living intelligently with one's surroundings, the same phenomenon holding true for psychological as well as physical exchanges.

   Chemical exhalation is an automatic, unconscious, routine, good-neighborly participation in the life cycle of living beings or, one could say, in the social milieu in which one lives: it is one aspect of good equilibrium in the overall ecological network.

- *a personal construct* – **a creation**: this is what makes us happiest, because we give something to the world, we contribute to its shaping and help it advance. It is that little bit extra, given by me – Joe Smith – that could not have been contributed by anyone else. If Smith had not been there, it would never have happened, at least not quite in that way – Smith-style.

   We have a certain pride then, a sense of accomplishment and joy; we feel alive in creating "that which has emerged from my very own personal ingenuity" and this in light of the ingenuity of others, their propositions, and the evolution of the world.

To Sum Up. Psychologists and psychoanalysts can be mistaken in seeing this problem incompletely, only considering the half of it. In fact, when they speak of introversion and extroversion:

- They may diagnose a fixed condition when what is happening is, in fact, the blockage of a movement.

- The solution they envisage – find a right mid-point between introversion and extroversion – is a mistake. There is no right mid-point!

Even when one stops talking about a right mid-point and one

recommends finding "a balance" between these two "faults" (extroversion and introversion), one is proposing a false image of what must be sought, for it evokes some ideal position between two extremes.

The right procedure is **to re-set into motion the alternance of introversion/extroversion**, not by wanting to find some good balance in-between the two tendencies but, on the contrary, by **looking for the maximum amplitude of one position or the other**, without getting stuck in it for too long and without becoming rigid about it. In other words, it is the swing of the pendulum, the respiratory process, of thought and action.

Position 1: I am being informed, I am penetrated by the outer world. Others have acted on me.

Position 2: I express myself, I breathe out, I counter-penetrate the outer world. I make my mark; I inject it with my personal ingenuity and act on others.

Position 1b: Others act on me, I am penetrated by a flow of information coming from outside.

Position 2b: I am going to gather my energy to "counter-react", express myself, despite the pressures from outside.

This to-and-fro movement of our pendulum will take place tirelessly if our internal rhythms and suppleness allow it and if they have been trained to that end. It is the weaver's shuttle passing from one hand to another on the loom, but it will stop weaving whenever it is held back by a cramped, rigid hand.

That which is tiring, that which constitutes sickness or neurotic tendency, is the pendulum getting stuck at one of the extremities of its swing. This is exhausting because a pendulum has a spontaneous tendency to invert its movement once it reaches the end of its course and to return to the opposite position.

The psychotherapist, or perhaps the doctor or wise counselor, who says to someone who thinks too much: "Run, do some sport, get your body moving, that's what you're lacking" is heading in the right direction. This is common sense and provides essential and immediate help – the gift of awakening the person to an easy "mechanical" unblocking.

The person so-advised will tell him, at the first opportunity: "It's quite silly really, but after running, getting my body to work, pruning my trees, digging up the weeds, and wheelbarrowing earth, I did feel an awful lot better – released somehow from my obsessions."

Likewise, the opposite advice can be given to the always-active extrovert: "Get some paper and write, open a Bible, and reflect a bit; go and sit in a church or sanctuary and gather yourself. Force yourself to contemplate, meditate, for a little while."

The agitated extrovert will feel better for it and will tell you: "That retreat I went on really did me some good" or, "Five minutes of reflection and meditation, from time to time; not bad at all!" Maybe they will say: "I had forgotten all about prayer but it *is* a good technique" or, "Stopping everything on the Sabbath – I had gotten out of the habit of doing it, but now I've taken it up again and feel all the better for it."

Dozens of ways exist to help you rediscover the alternant position that is missing from your life: the one that will set you back in balance once you re-find it. It is a question of balance through alternance and not of finding a "balance-point" or "suitable mid-point".

Let us repeat and insist upon our former statement: **There is no right mid-point**; there is no "good-balance". The "right mid-point" kills. Seeking a good balance (in the way usually prescribed) diminishes, annihilates, paralyses, and rusts our life-reflexes. There is an ongoing need for us to make the fabric of our lives progress – and life's fabric is only woven through alternances, like the movements of the shuttle in the weaver's hands.

There is still the problem of this movement's rhythm and amplitude. Here, let us not get too mathematical and let us try to avoid the norms of the absolute; rather, let us keep a few images in mind.

One image: that of these majestic old grandfather-clocks, still to be found in some old farmhouses, with their mighty pendulums, slow, tireless, and indestructible. They ring the hour, the half-hour, and the quarters with deep and confident tones that resonate through the house.

Then there are these other, smaller, faster-ticking timepieces that the Swiss make, where the hours and half-hours are marked by the sudden apparition of a little bird who tells you "cuckoo". His slightly piercing, rather grating, cry can also be heard throughout the house. There are also other, electric, clocks which mark the hours and the passage of time in silence: that is another style.

Also, there are the great church clocks which ring the hours and tell the time for a whole village. These are the equivalent of collective alternances, which have repercussions and resonance for us as individuals too.

Such images are so far removed from the arid, unresonant terms "extroversion and introversion", which can dry up one's life if the rigid diagnosis becomes fixed in one's mind. Whereas, with the freedom of reaction that alternance gives, one ought to be able to say to oneself, in the most natural and joyful way in the world: "How time passes!"

In the above way, extroversion and introversion are seen as moments which have overly prolonged themselves and that have not known the **swing of alternance**, which could have let them swing back and forth, periodically, with good timing, according to the individual and their type of personality.

Find the Exact Beat (Rhythm) of Alternance – Not the Exact Mid-Point. This is particularly a need for those who are sometimes somber and "locked up in themselves", and sometimes impatiently and explosively hyperactive. Those around them say that they have their "moods" and that they are temperamental. Psychiatrists call them "cyclothymic", seeing in these behavior changes shifts from a depressive phase to a hypomanic phase.

When they are excited, they are given tranquilizers and when they are "depressed", stimulants. This treatment can often aggravate the imbalance, for what they need, in general, is neither calming down nor stimulating, but accelerating: they are people who are late with respect to their own personal alternance cycle.

They are unbalanced not because they go through behavior changes but because these changes do not occur at the right moment, that is, at the time when the person needs them. This is because, being afraid of their own condition which has been presented to them as sickness, they are all the time putting the brakes on.

They thus become perpetually late with respect to themselves. When at last the movement is inversed, the pendulum, which has been held back in a wrong position, swings violently to the extreme opposite counter-position to compensate.

Children Said To Be Unstable. I am thinking now of the children brought to me because they are unstable. In class, they fidget on their seats, unable to sit quietly. At home, they run wild, unable to remain calm.

In my office they are the same, fidgeting on their chair and being told to behave by their parents. I immediately set up a situation, a rule, by giving them three chairs, allowing them to change from one to the other as much as they want. Already, after a dozen or so changes, they feel much better. A better atmosphere has been established.

For them it is, first-off, no one is bothering them any more for not staying seated on "their chair". They feel better because I provided them with a little alternance which acted as a safety-valve for whatever repressions they experience.

Obviously these children will not be cured simply because I have let them move about but the experience has already demonstrated that they can be improved "by mechanical means" – by getting them an extra chair to meet their need for movement.

And Those Seated Adults! This ties in with those adults that I teach to accelerate instead of braking: those to whom I explain that **alternance is life** but that they must discover this for themselves.

Let us say a word or two about the current way people sit in offices! That static, awful, attitude leads one to say, "Sit down, I have to talk with you" as if one could not talk while walking! Too many people have lost the habit of conversing, of finding concentration and of being serious, in any other way than sitting.

Be Obsessed but Alternating

We know the world has changed more in recent years than in millennia. Even nature, which traditionally we thought of as so vast, stable, and immeasurable, has been altered: its balances have been modified, sometimes lost, and nature itself is in threat of extinction. Amid all these external changes, only humanity has not fundamentally changed. No radical transformation has occurred in our ways of thinking or reasoning. Our models and behavior remain more or less as they have always been.

In order to get off the beaten track, one needs to know how to "be obsessed" – and not be afraid that, because of the obsessiveness, one is seen as being a bit "crazy" – only a bit, that is the difficult part. The restrictions and habit patterns all around us act like ready-laid tracks, ready-made grooves; back into which everything is pulling us. In order to get our wheels out of these deep, slippery ruts, we need constantly to give the steering of our life some sharp sideways twists, each immediately followed by a straightening-up. Should the wheels slip back in, then one needs to continue striving relentlessly to get them out, until a sufficient degree of progress is reached and a new course can be held.

The great psychiatrists Freud, Moréno, and Adler enabled us to discover certain mechanisms. Unfortunately others, less great, have leadened these by fixing them into rigid categories, nay catechisms, defined once and for all. Obsessives hold a prime place in these pre-defined categories.

Obsession is considered by far too many psychiatrists to be an ailment, or at least a failing, when, in actual fact, it represents the only mental way we have at present – as far as I know – of getting out of the ruts of traditional life and thinking, now often out-of-date and inadequate.

I challenge you, through reason and logical thinking, to get free from the ready-made ruts of your life without being obsessive. Look around and you will see the proof of this. Great people, those who make history, those in the news, the success stories, all have a sort of obsessive genius; certain of them so much so – for example, some artists or "mad scientists" – that they are even referred to as really sick, as paranoiacs.

When one does drive off the traditional routes, certain limits must not be exceeded. Psychiatrists are there to help point these out because, of course, one must avoid real craziness and the sort of anti-social reactions that would cause one to be put away. However, psychiatrists can cause harm when they hold us back too much, stopping us from being crazy enough to evolve – stopping us from being solidly obsessed but in a way which alternates!

That is the "trick" to get to know, the rhythm to recognize in oneself, to then cultivate and make into a habit. Then what could be a sterile, fixating obsession becomes something dynamic and enjoyable, helping one to maintain a forward thrust with a minimum of effort.

In fact, one must be aware that there exists a fundamental difference between, say, the obsessive fear of meeting spiders which paralyses one with horror and whatever it is that makes one kill them with violent blows, a difference poorly perceived by analysts. More than this, there is a radical difference between a fixed, centralized, single idea which ends up impoverishing life and "obsessional capital" which is rich in development and novelty.

"Always obsessed" is what people say to those with such capital who, in reply, can safely say: "Yes, it's true, but I've already changed my obsession three times since we last met." The art is to know how to play all of that like the keys of a piano, to weave the tunes of life.

Before becoming a virtuoso, you must first know how to play lesser pieces which are without pretension but sufficiently varied to get you into the habit of change, of alternating from one obsession to the other. It is remaining in the one obsession which brings the sterility.

Welcome the changes, even the ruptures, knowing how to sometimes close the piano by slamming the lid shut. Getting into the habit of accepting severances as normal events which further your life, thinking, and evolution, then you can treat yourself to a single obsessive phase of continuity, of mental follow-up, which will itself be alternant with the following phase.

This completes a small cycle, convenient and effective, which allows one to situate things more clearly, both within oneself and with others, when confronted with a hyper-logical society, one which can seem unbearable at times and exalting at others.

Hold your ground without being devoured and without feeling the need to devour others. Hold on by weaving your very own fabric, by playing that piece of music which is your very own life, staying as close as can be to who you fundamentally are. Do it by impulse, not by clenching your teeth all the time, nor too often sailing into the wind with only will for a motor. This does not preclude the occasional education of will, as long as it is not continuous.

Sailing – the use of spontaneous air currents with a minimum of added effort and the emergence of a fine intelligence of situational components, the gusts of wind and calms – offers much and, amid the increasing din of motors, is very likely to become a compensating sport for a growing number of people.

To make use of our inner impulses, our imagination, and our good obsessive tendencies and to favor these amid the social currents – that is sailing.

One very particular instance, in this analogy, is to learn to use only the storm jib and not the mainsail when strong winds oblige.

Obsession, then, can be a personal means of extricating oneself, with determination, from the one-way tracks laid down by society and routine. In the present context, it is good to know how to welcome obsessions, how to give priority to new ones, how not to make old ones into routines, and how not to get set in one's ways. From this point of view, break-off and start-off points are life's essential moments: Allowing large sections of the past to be filed away in one's subconscious, these points are both useful and structuring.

Then is the coming back, like Ulysses after his magnificent journey, to another part of one's life, which now is allowed to be full of break-offs and restarts; back to the continuum, perhaps – but that, in itself, can give one the means, the blueprint, for rediscovery and orienting one's impulses. Alternating obsession with the continuum constitutes, in fact, skillful management of oneself within social life.

Some Relevant Examples

Surveying the patients I have treated in my thirty years of medical practice, I notice that almost all of them who were socially important or highly successful profited from a basic obsessive streak. In most cases, the way I could help was to make it easier for them to alternate, either between their current obsession and the next one (usually already peeking over the horizon) or between their new obsession and an old one that was coming again to the surface. The following snatches of dialogue should give the general idea.

> **Patient**: "I hardly dare admit it, doctor, but all the enthusiasm I had for my project when I saw you last, and all that concentration, putting myself body and soul into it and turning all my colleagues onto it – well, it's all gone now!"
> **Dr** (*pretending to be astounded and a little worried*): "Ah?"
> **P.** (*looking somber and guilty*): "Yes, the momentum is gone and I'm having to really push myself. I'm trying to work out some plan of action to be able to follow through with it all."
> **Dr**: "Ah! But surely there are people working with you to take care of everything, aren't there?"
> **P.**: "Yes, thank goodness."
> **Dr**: "So your lack of enthusiasm doesn't show on the surface?"
> **P.** (*worried*): "I hope not."
> **Dr**: "Well then, since nobody knows about the way you feel and since things are getting on OK without you in fact, then, as I know you, you've surely got some new idea brewing?"
> **P.** (*suddenly brighter and full of life*): "Well, between you and me, there is. I barely dare speak of it – even to admit it to myself, but there is an idea fermenting inside me. I'm really taken by it – can't sleep at nights thinking of it . . ."

There we go, off again into another obsession, for a week or a month.

Within this context of an obsession either following another one or switching back into an old one, I have dealt with hundreds of cases, helping the persons concerned to alternate without guilt. In so doing, I would always listen critically to the camouflage mechanisms that they felt obliged to set up in order not to be attacked by a society which stresses continuity. In general, this help proved stimulating and very efficient.

The cases varied from a great industrial innovator, head of a massive workforce, to a solitary inventor who could barely even confide in his wife who was a little embittered because they had no money. In between were all the others – obsessed with manual work, stamp-collecting, video-films, this, that and all the other obsessions that we, each of us, have as part of ourselves at certain times or in certain aspects of our life.

The essential thing is for each of us:

1. Not to think ourselves crazy because we are obsessed;
2. To know how to shift from one obsession to another, without guilt;
3. To burst out laughing when someone treats us as obsessives;
4. To nevertheless know when it is time to alternate by welcoming in the next obsession.

In so doing, we live joyously, efficiently, and actively instead of thinking ourselves sick.

Order and Disorder

Order is often contrasted with disorder, not with the idea that they can alternate but rather as a way of making the one seem a virtue and the other a fault. This is a serious mistake which does us considerable disservice and it will continue to do so until both order and disorder are clearly and appropriately integrated within us.

First, let us approach this question of order and disorder through what is commonly thought and generally said about it. One frequently hears it said of someone that they have their good points and their bad points. If they are talking about a very organized person, this could imply that he or she may somewhat lack imagination, which we know to be refreshingly creative.

"The mess I work in, but somehow I feel at home in it . . . "

"His disorder, which only he understands . . . "

These are the sorts of things that people say as well and they suggest that disorder is not quite so disorganized as all that, at least for the person who has created it. Disorder can be stimulating when it occurs as something temporary. When it is the status quo, it is often tiring, dispersing our concentration and energy.

We all know people who scream the moment one touches their things in the hope of tidying them up. Maybe you the reader are like that yourself. The wife who tidies up everything (after which the husband can never find anything) is a well-known phenomenon. The reverse is possible as well, and perhaps devoutly wished for by many a working mother. In either case, the situation is often the cause of family squabbles.

"Leave me alone in my untidiness; it suits me fine"

"Above all, don't let anyone go into my bedroom"

are typical phrases that some use to defend their particular chaos.

I remember a brilliant attorney that I had to treat at one point. One day, with great mystery, she took me into her home then took out a high security key and, before opening the door to her bedroom, said:

"I'm going to let you in where no one else has ever been, even my closest friends. You won't believe your eyes. I'm not ashamed of it, for no one has ever seen it, but sometimes I find myself worrying that one day, because of some emergency, a fire maybe, the fire-brigade, or the police will be obliged to break the door down, enter and discover it all. That is maybe part of the reason that I am showing it to you now and that I put myself, in some ways, in your hands."

I was intrigued. The door opened. She went in first and said, "Be careful, you have to make your way through things." Sideways on, I had still not seen anything. The next second, I found myself in a bedroom strewn with files and loose leaves bearing only odd hastily-scribbled words.

I understood it instantly to be a "structured disorder", her own personal disorder. She could move through it like a girl playing hop-scotch, setting down a foot in the odd places that had stayed empty. She could maneuver freely, taking advantage of each step to shift a file, pick up a sheet of paper and put it on the bedside table or some other piece of furniture.

As for me, I found it harder to move around. It was not "my disorder". She thought it was proper to explain to me, as a way of excusing the mess, that in this she never forgot what she ought to be thinking about and that it was, effectively, her way of working. She felt me to have immediately understood something essential about it that she herself could not put her finger on and so continued, saying:

"In fact, all this is the basis for my work-method – if it's right to talk about work-methods when referring to such a mess. Anyway, for me it's a must. Every time I tried to set things in order, I ended up wasting an enormous amount of energy on things which, before in their 'normal' stated, used to lead into each other quite naturally and become obvious when the time was ripe."

What she needed to hear was the idea of structured disorder; the life-environment that one modifies and remodels constantly.

An image came to mind – that of old barns and old worksheds that no one has been in or worked in for a long, long time and where spiders' webs and dust testify to the occupant's absence. But there what is most striking of all is the absence of life, that characteristic so peculiar to things which are dead or have lain idle.

Two other images might also be introduced at this point: one is that of the spinner whose intelligent, hard-working hands pull on the tow, making the movements which twist and create the thread; the other is that of the relics of spinning wheels and weaving looms, totally devoid of any life, that one finds in museums.

Had the young woman fallen ill or had she been temporarily absent from her home for a few weeks, her room strewn with living, pre-occupying documents would have progressively become like an old attic in which one finds, with astonishment or melancholy, the testimony of what once was a life, an occupation.

I continued, "You really could use a social key for your lack of order: a way to arrange things so that, should some indiscretion occur, you will be completely whitewashed, totally vindicated. Just suppose you fall ill and someone has to bring you home."

"That is precisely what often worries me, although I've never formulated it clearly before now," she exclaimed.

This is the key that I had made for her. Others would have been equally suitable. "Take a large sheet of drawing paper and write, in huge letters with a marking-pen: WEEKLY SORTING OUT ON BEDROOM FLOOR. Beneath that you make three sub-headings:

1. Original confidential briefs and manuscripts to be kept here.
2. Things currently being classified – with pleas.
3. Files and documents to go to secretary.

Put that somewhere where it can be seen, with marker-pens alongside, in such a way that absolutely no one will fail to notice it immediately. Then you write anything else you want, it doesn't really matter. It gives a very normal explanation of what is going on to anyone coming into the room. It may even happen that you will start to make use of the false chart yourself, to take a step forward in your own handling of this disorder in case you want to shift objects according to their movement and position in your mind."

She suddenly started laughing and said, "I know I'm going to seem even crazier but, since I know that you can understand, I'll tell you something else. Believe it or not, I might get married, now that you've had a visit here to see this, because for me this was a serious obstacle that I only half admitted to: I had no idea how to present this chaos to a normal and well-ordered man."

We barely saw each other after my visit to her place. We had started out from the periphery of her personality at the time of her first medical consultations. I no longer know why she originally came to see me: maybe unexplainable or recurring stomach-aches; maybe twinges in the throat, a periodic hoarseness that she was scared would crop up on the day that she had to present her plea. What difference does it make?

Our medical relationship had, step by step, made headway into the deeper layers of her anxiety and personality. This to the point where it touched deep enough to reach what was really pre-occupying her, the thing she revealed to no one, not even totally to herself: the secret disorder of her bedroom floor. As with the end of a cycle, things suddenly wound themselves up. She might have changed to another doctor or simply stopped having a need for a doctor at all, perhaps for a long time.

To know how to open the door on your own disorder. To know how to close it behind you. Then to know how to live in the order imposed by others, for a short while or longer, if that suits your temperament or if you are obliged to do so. Then the door again; the key you turn in the lock in order to get back into your own life but always, at a certain point, by going through a phase of disorder.

For some the only way of coping with disorder is through crisis. Sometimes they smash everything. For others, it is the opposite: having to set things in order represents the crisis. All that is very natural, normal, and desirable.

What is abnormal is to be a little too disordered, or so over-ordered that one becomes irritating to others. If you happen to be abnormally ordered or disordered then, from a social point of view, the important thing is not to show others the fraction that is excessive. Our young advocate, in the very particular disorder she maintained in her bedroom (which was really her creative space), must have felt the instinctive need to preserve her public image, so she locked the bedroom door.

A jumble of objects, momentarily piled up, is different from those heaps which remain to sag and fade with time because there is no one to remodel them, use them, or give them life. Another image is that of jugglers, who often whirl and twirl a very odd assortment of objects, which they catch and re-launch until the show stops and everything is restored to order, grouped in their hands and then thrown to the assistant who puts it all into a basket.

Disorder can rise, if it is very well maintained, to such a sophisticated degree that it ends up giving the impression of order. Modern biophysics gives us a vivid example of this in the apparent disorder of molecules, incessantly on the move.

Nature itself, viewed globally, astounds us with the general harmony that it displays, because it works as a whole and works well. That is what is astounding, for when one looks a little closer, one observes what seems to be total disorder. Animals are in conflict, one with another, and fight in territorial battles. Micro-animals, the microbes, do the same thing. It all seethes in the most unlikely way. Man has wanted to impose his sort of order into it all and we realize today that the attempt has not always been his most glorious accomplishment.

When we predominantly make use of either order or disorder in our lives, it makes a lot of sense not to present others with an image which is disturbed or disturbing. This general opinion of disorder crops up, by the way, in the following instance, which is very striking when one thinks about it: when the Bible talks of chaos, the word is generally understood as derogatory and taken to mean a situation that must be resolved as quickly as possible.

Chaos, however, could be seen as an initial disorder which was then structured, to again be de-structured, then re-structured, and so forth. Chaos, therefore, need not be a bad thing in itself but a phase.

Order and disorder: Which is the positive quality and which the fault? For a positive quality carried to extremes is a fault; and a fault seen as a phase could be a necessity, a helpful thing.

One might wonder why human activity (like that of animals and all that lives in nature) tends to be organizing. We will discuss this in a book written in conjunction with Arnold Kaufmann, the mathematician, exploring human ingenuity when it is faced with the forces of natural degradation.

Put men in the desert and they will build pyramids. Let the wind blow for a few millennia: only dust then remains. Put men in the desert again and they will re-build the pyramids.

Order and disorder, this endless alternance, is the whole of life.

Order and Disorder: The Mail Nightmare

My office (or my desk) is in a state of disorder; I resent myself for letting it get that way. This is another very common situation which, if wrongly interpreted or badly timed, can be quite painful, engendering an inner feeling of guilt. This can be detrimental in cases where one gets fixated on an isolated image of disorder without thinking about the radical tidy-ups and sort-outs which form its necessary complement.

An office that is *always disordered*, never tidied, can lead to serious inconveniences (penalties for being overdue, loss of official or important documents) and this becomes a materially dangerous state of affairs in our present-day world. It is not at all the same situation when that same office is, from time to time, tidied up. Those "time to time" efforts provide alternance and balance out the disorder sufficiently for problems to be avoided.

Momentary disorder is generally due to a backlog of paperwork onto which is piled the incoming, current lot; we refuse to classify these papers as fast as they appear because that would distract, bore, and tire us uselessly.

I have often treated people suffering from nausea (a rejection reflex) brought on by the bureaucratic work that our present highly administration-oriented society imposes. These unhappy individuals feel so guilt-ridden that they pass by their desk hardly daring to look at it, just slipping the latest piece of paper received on top of the pile, to "deal with it tomorrow".

They thus live in a state of perpetual imbalance, due to the threat posed by the burden of all those unsorted, undealt-with papers. Some lose sleep over it. Yet it does not take much to restore the mental balance and, more particularly, to enable them to feel at home in their disorder rather than to be afraid of it – to live with it in an active and blameless way while ensuring, nevertheless, that certain minimum safeguards are maintained.

The following plan has given my patients very good results:

A. Disorder is to be unreservedly accepted.

B. However, we (the patient and therapist) make an agreement that every letter will be opened and dealt with, using a series of reflex safety procedures.

These procedures are:

1. The letter is opened.
2. If it is advertising material, it is immediately thrown in the waste paper bin.
3. If it is personal, official, tax, business, or friendly correspondence, then it can be read or not (does not matter) but must be treated in the following, obligatory, way:

   a. The envelope is stapled to the letter.
   b. If an answer is required by a certain date, the date is immediately marked in a personal pocket diary.

   c. The reply needed is made there and then, so as to get the
      matter off one's back. It can be done later if, for instance,
      the letter balks, worries, saddens, or angers; in that case, it
      is sometimes better to consider one's response awhile. That
      is a different problem which ought not get tangled up with
      these minimum security measures.

There is another safety measure: not to empty the waste paper bins
daily, as is often done. Then the subconscious has the *material*
certainty that nothing can be mistakenly chucked and so no serious
mistake will occur on that level.

The disorder is still there but now without the burden of threat
added to it. The situation becomes quite different, allowing blitz tidy-
ups to be gestures of alternance rather than desperate, exhausting
moments in which:

1. One no longer remembers clearly when the letter arrived
   (because its date-stamped envelope has been tossed);
2. One finds out, in horror, that the "reply-by" date is imminent
   or has passed;
3. One of the papers in the envelope is now missing (in our plan,
   everything was systematically stapled, or placed together in a
   plastic cover, so nothing can ever be missing);
4. By mistake, vital papers have been discarded – not emptying
   the bin daily helps safeguard against this.

The above systematic steps may seem childish. Nevertheless, some
of my patients have had miracle cures simply through putting these
minimum safeguards into practice (they no longer need tranquilizers
or sleeping-tablets). They were able to consciously feel at home with
their disorder, knowing it to be the second facet of an alternance.
Disorder was no longer an insoluble defect that needed to be fought
against.

Appreciate the advantages of your disorder – without a guilt
complex. Only reply, for instance, to preoccupying mail in liberating
intense bursts of writing, in moments of alternance, rather than
poisoning yourself with it day after day. "Poisoning oneself" – how
accurate that saying is. Those kinds of methodical obligations,
inexorable and continuous, are really poison for certain types of
temperament. That needs to be seriously considered.

There are little details of daily life that can gradually sap you and
which, accumulating and being there day after day, can constitute a

considerable burden or bring on a state of depression.

Always bear the contrasting state of affairs in mind, so you are able to accept it when it happens and thereby put yourself back in balance: be aware that one day or another you will have to go through it when, in a panic, you will be obliged to set the situation straight.

Once these things are being done, disorder can assume its positive aspect. It offers considerable possibilities to the intuition, which will learn with increasing flair how to spot the interesting things emerging from disorder. Often they just seem to fall into one's hands "as if by chance".

Actually, there are very few people who are either totally organized or totally disorganized. Much more common is for someone to be either a little too much one way or the other and to feel guilty about it.

If you are very organized, perhaps even extremely fussy, accept it with a smile and without getting uptight about those moments of disorder; they add the spice to life because they are life's natural alternances. Learn to laugh at your shortcomings, even to the point of liking them as positive qualities – at least as living, authentic manifestations of your personality.

Creative Disorder: "What a Lovely Mess This Is!"

Innovation has two main elements: creation and realization. Whereas it is order which makes the realization of an idea possible, it is out of disorder that the specific moment of creation, the spark of genius, will emerge. Creation takes place in disorder: this is little recognized and sometimes disputed. One could imagine hearing a comment like the following:

"Yes, he's brilliant, it's true, but if only he were not so disorganized and didn't leave such a mess, that total confusion, then what he could create would be phenomenal!" It is extremely tempting to want to make innovators perfect, to turn them into "inventing machines".

I remember well the case of an industrialist from Lyon, who produced printed fabrics and silken goods. He had discovered a man in Paris, somewhere in that extraordinary post-war ferment in the Latin Quarter; he had at one point studied fine art and was, at the time, keeping himself alive by doing odd jobs. On the back of a bistro napkin, this man had sketched ingenious patterns of amazing freshness and novelty. These were infinitely better than those produced by the industrialist's team of designers, back in his Lyon studios, who were stuck in their routine.

Though they had just met by chance one evening, the industrialist immediately thought he should sign up this man. Instead of a bistro napkin to sketch on, he would have a magnificent designer's studio to work in, with several people under him to copy the creations he could produce day after day. Yes, but . . .

Once at Lyon, in his sumptuously fitted-out workshop, this fellow, whose genius had clearly shown itself in those casual sketches, became incapable of producing anything better than the other designers. If anything, he was worse than they, for they at least were used to routine and being methodical.

I happened to be aware of all the details of this case because the young man in question, who had become sterile as far as design was concerned, was driven to the point of illness by his incapacity. His boss, who was a patient of mine, had advised him to consult me. It took me some time to understand in depth the reason why this artist's inspiration had dried up when he shifted to a lifestyle and work conditions which, if anything, should have given free rein to his productivity and genius.

"I have everything I need to be happy, to be efficient, yet nothing comes of it. I just produce third-rate trash," he told me. It was only later, during the second or third consultation, that the reality of his situation came to light.

"Actually, I'm bored in this magnificent design-studio and in my ultra-modern apartment. Nothing is inspiring. After a few weeks in this new set-up I was drained, emptied out. Funny – I have everything necessary to be in top form. The boss even suggested I make use of his pool, if I feel like relaxing. I end up feeling I was better off in my attic in Paris. At least there I was able to come up with inspired designs within minutes, on the back of a paper tablecloth."

We gradually came to understand what was happening by looking at the situation in the new light shed by this fact: his creative capacities were more or less inversely proportional to his standard of living. The incredible muddle in which he had previously lived and the setbacks that he had to cope with then represented an infinitely superior "richness of life". As for the alternances which rained on him, one after another, they were incessant.

He came to realize that all of his brilliant ideas had nearly always occurred to him in odd and varied places – rarely when sitting in front of his drawing-board. The vital elements of his creativity were: the richness of his (the inventor's) life, constant rupture of the continuum, alternances thrust upon him by circumstance, and the non-symmetrical, bizarre, quirky character of a setting in which new ideas could surface and unfold.

We agreed that he should come to see me for a number of 8-day periods of intensive psychotherapy. In the beginning it was necessary to do the spadework on the case, using non-conventional techniques. Next I had to give him the possibility of finding his ideal work conditions again. This was sometimes on the bus, on his way to see me, or in my waiting room (which is tiny), or a railway platform, subway bench, or waiting in line at the cinema but never in his custom-equipped drawing-office. No one ever knew anything of what we had cooked up: he would return from Paris with dozens of sketches on assorted scraps of paper from which he could then draw up proper designs.

The case which I have just outlined is a clear example of the fact that not only are order and disorder intimately related to the psychological mechanisms of innovation but, also, that alternance between the two will enable invention to go through two significant phases: first comes the genius of creation in the midst of disorder and chance setbacks; then there is the material realization which requires some organization.

The explanation of creation through disorder lies in the creativity of the unconscious mind. When one is isolated in an office, it is the conscious mind which acts and creativity is brought to a halt if there is a lack of alternance between the conscious and unconscious.

The error of judgment made by the industrialist from Lyon was to put our artist into the inexorable order of a model design office: this had the effect of making his work sterile. As soon as the artist got back into alternance between order and disorder, his creative genius was able to show itself again.

Neither Robot nor Savage

As life these days steers us along its fixed tracks, it more or less "robotizes" us. When observing, in reality or on film, crowds moving in stations at rush-hour or in the city streets, one is often struck by the thought, "Gosh, they look just like robots!" It makes many of us think, of course, of Charlie Chaplin's "Modern Times".

We quickly shun the idea that we ourselves are, at times, one of those robots. The mere thought of it makes us dream of becoming savages again, able to act on our emotions and the instincts of the moment.

But then, does anyone truly wish to be either robot or savage?

The play of alternance between these two aspects of our lives – automatism and the desire to rediscover the savage's spontaneity – is very interesting. It can help us better understand the frequent clashes that occur between our instinctive tendencies and our duties.

Who has not dreamt of being surrounded by a vast array of mechanical slaves that would take care of every uninteresting task while we deal with all the nobler actions – creation, invention, and change? This robot vision, however, has its downside. To be surrounded solely by mechanical robots (or robotized humans) would be to live in a world without imagination, a world where one could well end up becoming a robot oneself. There would be too much of the pre-planned and, in the end, it would be thoroughly boring, perhaps even unbearable.

The "savage" represents the other magnetic pole of our behavior: he is instinctive, hypersensitive, gifted with extra-sensory perceptions, capable of giving vent to his moods, of leaping, of yelping with joy, of being immediately content to live out the instant for whatever it is, good or bad – wherever, in a paradisiacal garden or on a dusty, rocky road.

The noble savage theory is linked to this tendency: the total shedding of the civilized, the sophisticated, the pre-planned, and reason so that one can instead plunge into nature, amid animals, ferns, hills, and forests.

When undergoing the shocks and counter-shocks of life, each one of us dreams of the savage – and perhaps of the robot too – in different ways but with the following limitations:

- extreme pre-planning takes us too far into the mechanical, the repetitive, the unimaginative, and the "totally pre-programmed";
- the wildness of the savage takes us too far into the uncontrolled, into mood swings, and moves which are purely instinctual and frenzied. It is the perpetual gust of wind which ends up by instilling in us the need for a port to be built to shelter us from its blast. We feel linked to the origins of civilization, given that many of its inventions are made to precisely that end - a retreat from the wild state.

What to do, then, with these instinctive and contradictory tendencies which we feel, at certain moments, surging up in ourselves, sometimes as the magnetism of myth and sometimes as the draw of a cozy, creative haven, freed from routine, repetitious tasks?

Must we suppress these tendencies and file them away forever in the cabinet marked "impossible, time-consuming, and energy-wasting utopias"? From a medical point of view, I must say I have known all sorts of cases and options, from those who have decided to revert to the wild to those who have shut up their dreams and wildness in a cupboard but who have also, at one point of heroic decision, thrown the cabinet key down into a deep well so as never to be tempted to use it again.

The ensuing drama then becomes this: even though the person can no longer open their cupboard, the temptation to do so still remains with them, the lingering feeling of lost opportunity that they will never have again. My role, as a physician, has often been to help such people get their key back from the bottom of the well.

Through the idea of alternance, it becomes clearer and less complicated. In any case, it becomes something accessible; something we can realize through special brief interludes – somewhat like those refreshing moments, those whiffs of fresh air, that we all learn to create for ourselves, whatever our lifestyle.

With wildness comes the alarming possibility of uncontrollable, exuberant madness. With the robot comes the solely-mechanical, which might be compared to nailing all imagination, every change, and any creativity into a coffin.

For those who prefer the prepared, the foreseen, the ready-formulated, the sort of life where the robot has its place, wildness might be the weekend break. The "Saturday-night drunkenness syndrome" is a social illustration of this mechanism – with this rider, however: it would be better to have this weekly moment of wildness without having to get drunk.

Those who prefer the unforeseen, finding it neither disconcerting nor scattering, will feel happy in an unstructured life and will feel capable of absorbing their life-food as it comes, without needing it to be pre-digested by one of our modern systems of "life-processing" (like word-processing in computers). The oscillations of change can be an integrating factor in the lives of these more "unorganized" personalities.

These few explanations and this outline help us understand the degree to which alternance can make all the possibilities in life much more accessible. As far as maximum oscillations or major swings are concerned, they will no longer appear as taboos provoking neurosis or as frustrations which make us groan and cry only to then seek out some artificial paradise – or a psychiatrist.

Let us seek and find our balance and natural dynamism in alternance between these two opposing tendencies, represented by the robot and the wild man. This should be done in the clear knowledge that those two are the extremities of the swing, the two "sanity barriers" that must not be crossed.

Between these two extremes – which we should allow ourselves to enjoy without guilt, lucidly, and whenever circumstances permit – we find everything we need in order to live and oscillate while still maintaining a general direction of life which is as close as possible to our heart's desires.

Some Relevant Examples

What doctor is unaware of how dramatic life is for those who have been carried so far into living like a robot that they can no longer get out of it or for those who have gone so far in expressing the wild part of their personality that they can no longer socialize or fit in with the social circumstances around them? My whole career as a doctor, as I am sure is the case for many other doctors, has been spent in helping the "robots" be a little less mechanical and to make a series of swings towards spontaneity as well as in helping the "savages" become a little more systematic and a little less discordant in their life's activities.

Neither robot

> **Dr**: "Sir, you have just been telling me how overstretched you are at the office and unable to round off your work each day, so you end up taking it home with you to finish in the evening. Medically speaking, I must say I find you exhausted, overburdened and, quite frankly, at the end of your tether."
>
> **Patient**: "Yes, doctor, that's about it."
>
> **Dr**: "I'm prescribing the following treatment. First, here are some drops to take to help with the exhaustion: take them after work. Secondly, you must take an hour's walk after leaving the office each evening. Thirdly, I formally and medically forbid you to take work home with you."
>
> **P**: "But I'll never manage, doctor; I'm so behind with everything!"
>
> **Dr**: "OK then, it will have to be three weeks off work."
>
> **P**: "No! That's out of the question."
>
> **Dr**: "Very well then, you had better let all your colleagues know that you will be unable to take any work home with you over the coming month."

The next thing that the doctor must take into consideration is the necessity of giving the patient some way of externalizing the "wild" side of their personality after leaving work in the evening, rather than just continuing to be a robot. This might take the form of a moment's gardening or perhaps fishing for someone who lives in the country. One of my patients used to chop wood. Another, a distinguished student, took up French boxing and yet another took up karate; a woman might dance or paint.

Nor Savage. On the other hand, in cases of young people in wild revolt against society, it is possible to induce some behavioral improvement by getting them to repaint houses, wielding the paintbrush mechanically like a robot for hours on end. Through performing these methodical and automatic gestures they can, by the day's end, accomplish something tangible and visible on the walls, and they are often astonished at their own efficiency. In my experience, they were happy with what they had done for they were no longer confined to inefficient disorder.

There is the case of the "Bel Espoir": the boat where Father Jaouen subjected delinquents to a ship's daily work discipline. In America we have the example of groups of troubled teens sent on treks across desert regions, carrying their bags and equipment on mules. These are fairly obvious examples of induced alternance, making people do the opposite of what they normally would do – in this case, helping them accept the limits and rules of social adjustment, that is, something of the robot.

When robotized, find opportunities for being a little wild. When too wild, find activities sufficiently robotizing that they will educate the wildness. But always without reaching the point of being either a total robot or a total savage.

Profiles in Conflict: The Seagull and the Elephant

Many of life's difficulties seem to end up in a choice between these two extremes, with little or no possibility of some middle way. In our Western culture, flight is considered cowardice and those who run away are scorned whereas those who stay and fight are considered to have shown a worthwhile, exemplary reaction. Their reaction sometimes carries the additional risk of death. Whatever one may say, certain habitual ways of thinking are deeply embedded in our culture and, for the sake of human respect, unfortunate souls are often flung into useless and dangerous conflicts.

However, one can get out of such situations without losing face and without putting one's life at risk. We shall see how alternance can be of help in highlighting options which are much less stark: a wealth of intermediary solutions which manifest quite clearly.

Series of waves and counter-waves, one overlapping the other – surging surface waves and undercurrents that sweep all in their path – that is how life can seem once the wind is up. Confronted with that wind, birds present an extremely small surface-area of resistance: the degree to which their contours are aerodynamic is astonishing.

In a storm, which tears away at everything, taking the roofs of houses, ripping the trees from the coast and the masts from ships, the seagulls use the wind to soar and glide. But we are not gulls; nor shall we ever be.

We all see, among our acquaintances, those who, rather than reducing their profile when times get stormy, prefer instead to present more of their "surface", to stand up to and defy the wind. We probably have done the same ourselves on certain occasions, even if it was not the wisest of stances to adopt.

Using the idea of alternance consists of keeping two opposite attitudes well in mind:

1. Presenting a minimum profile, or
2. Facing up.

There are certain conflicts in the face of which it is impossible not to react: there are things which one feels one must oppose.

There will always be moments when one has to opt for one stance or the other: to be a bird who lets the wind slide by or the bear who ferociously blocks the entrance to his cave. The essential point is to have both images in mind in order to mentally alternate between the two, i.e., to choose with suppleness.

The person who always faces up to whatever it is, because he or she does not know or has never tried the other way of reacting, stands in great danger.

The person who always lets things slide past and never opposes anything does not realize that, sometimes at least, one must face up, stand up to things, and adopt the different stance. He or she shrinks and shrinks again and again in order not to have to fight, at the end of the day becoming nothing.

It is a great teaching and a great freedom to be able to switch at times to an opposite stance. By standing long enough in the shoes of the different way, sometimes the opposite way, of dealing with things, one is then at liberty to really choose what to do and can wisely take the right and appropriate decision for that situation.

- "I have decided to stand firm: it's time to react."
- "I have decided to let it flow by. I'll present the least possible surface area."

In nature, seagulls have no choice. Their lives are already determined by natural forces, by the winds that guide them. Likewise elephants, powerfully and heftily-built, have no choice. The elephant's life is one of barging ahead or, with their powerful trunk, clearing away anything in their path or opposed to them. They face up to things their whole life long, dominating and modeling their environment with the sheer bulk of their muscles. Only man has the choice of what to be, including deciding which of these two attitudes to adopt in a situation – that of the seagull or that of the elephant.

Of course, there also exist intermediate possibilities which are even better if, before making a choice, one has mentally alternated between the possibilities. One finds this in the expression "weighing up the pros and cons", the age-old application of common sense which does not mean fussing to find the "good compromise" or "right mid-point" which is so often, as we said before, a false concept.

Some Relevant Examples

Let us take the well known example of labor conflicts between workers and employers. When one officially takes the side of one or the other, in times of crisis, and gets into a face-to-face battle with fixed positions – that is the attitude of the elephant. Not to fight but instead to eclipse oneself in those circumstances and disappear into a crowd without stating an opinion, letting the wind slide past one's feathers – that is to adopt the attitude of the seagull.

Note that because of our Western socio-cultural habits which oblige people to fight in order to manifest their opinions, the latter stance could be considered as running away from the situation. It might be as well to reflect a little, at this point, on the fact that in nature more than half the animals owe their survival to an ability to flee, which is an integral part of their behavior-patterns.

It has become common to regard those who do stand up to situations, who assume tough responsibilities, as "real men" or as "iron ladies". However, when things turn for the worst and employees are sacked or companies go bust, there is often a spouse waiting to react to their now unemployed wife or husband: "Why did you have to get yourself so worked up, take a front-line position in the heart of the fray, and be so cussed about your principles?" (This is, of course, except when the other is also militant or someone having very firm opinions on the matter: then they would not have accepted anything other than what did happen.)

It is obviously not possible, in any of these situations, to determine your stance in advance. Alternance consists of first locating the two extreme attitudes possible and then alternating, mentally, between them in order to prepare oneself for taking the intelligent decision at the appropriate time.

It can be quite interesting to study some of the positions that people do take and one can do this by applying the contrasted imagery of the elephant and the seagull. I remember one case. Let us call it: "A seagull in the hospital while elephants battle."

It happened during the Algerian war at the time when the French generals refused to obey their government. They wanted to stay where they were and continue the fight, with the aid of their faithful troops. In the heart of it all was one senior officer who, at the most crucial moment of the crisis, when normally he would have been obliged to opt for one position or the other, happened to fall sick and was hospitalized. Whether his sickness was real or diplomatic, no one will ever know. However, when it came to settling accounts, the punishments and the military tribunals, he was not at all involved, having been officially unaware of what was going on outside his hospital ward. He had taken the stance of the gull even though he was in the elephants' camp.

It would be easy to say that that sort of person is an opportunist. But when it comes to politicians, one says that they are fine diplomats and that they know how to sail with the wind, an expression which cannot fail to remind us of birds.

The opposite stance is that of the ''bull in a china shop''. Between the two there is an intermediary attitude: that of the cat, capable of weaving slinkily between pieces of porcelain without breaking a thing. One does find, actually, in some social conflicts an intermediary tactic which shows some alternance. This is the case of the negotiators who, going from one camp to another, diplomatically adjust their sails to suit the wind of whichever camp they happen to be in. One could cite dozens of other examples and you certainly have some in and around your own life.

Whether we have the mental profile of the gull or the elephant, it is always extremely useful to clearly determine the opposite stance. Not as the mortal enemy but as the alternative attitude.

If your own life obliges you to play one or the other of these roles – presenting more surface to or sliding through the wind – you must make sure to be properly in phase with your alternances and not end up like those who always find themselves in the wrong camp: those who spend all their time in counter-rhythm and counter-situation. To escape the counter-rhythms, we need to learn to sense the waves of life. The alternance idea will help us with this.

The proverb says that it takes all sorts to make a world. In nature, the gull and the elephant each have their role and each have their place. Within human society, where we often have the opportunity to oscillate between the two positions and the possibility of a choice, then to be a gull at times and, at other times, an elephant is yet one more form of freedom.

The Joys of an Occasionally Imprecise Perfectionist

I remember a convention on communication. The point of it was to learn how to express yourself precisely and to concern yourself with what other people had understood through what you had said. This approach naturally involved the concept of verbal precision and immediately ruled out the use of any terms which might be considered "vague".

Paradoxically, the outcome of this convention on communication was that, within a very short space of time, no one was able to communicate with anyone else, except the convention leader who, in his guise of hunter of improper terminology and imprecise language, dealt out whiplashes of punishment upon each participant in turn, to chastise them back onto the precise path. Sound grotesque? It was.

This convention on "perfect communication" was an example, a model, of what should not be done. The proof was its outcome: no one was able to express anything to anyone and, if they did manage to do so, it was so slowly, so pre-scanned for error, and so bombastic that it became the very opposite of conversation, which hopefully conveys and transmits something. And the whole point of the convention was supposed to be communication!

What Happened? What Went Wrong?

All those "imperfections", the imprecisions and improper terms in each person's language and mode of expression, in fact represent a host of convenient devices enabling "the current to flow". That the only purpose of language is to be rigid and precise, like a mathematical theorem, has yet to be effectively demonstrated. The opposite is probably true.

All those words which have an implicit meaning for their speaker, yet are understood in some other way by different listeners, are **lingua franca**; what one might call "general-purpose" terms. They do not constitute a goal in themselves but enable the conversation to continue and come to its conclusion. In the end, these general purpose words have merely served as bridges enabling one to gain the other shore.

What are "general-purpose" words? They are the ones which are vague in meaning and imprecise.

Because the terms we use are at times imprecise and since that could lead, among other things, to excessive generalization, we might too hastily conclude that all vagueness needs to be vigorously outlawed.

The prime reason for language is so that people can express themselves and so that relationships can be established between individuals. Let that not be forgotten.

Furthermore, it is true that some aspects of language have acquired a precision that has proven extremely useful in certain domains. But that is all. Who would impose permanent precision, continuous and implacable "self-consciousness" in the use of language? Life itself, with its currents and very necessary suppleness, demands something other than that if we are not to be stifled and paralyzed by rigid austerity.

Thank goodness the traditional customs of language are there to bring a bit of common sense to these modern excesses. Often those who communicate the best turn out to be the least precise, the most woolly, but also the most pleasant people. These communicators, and everyone knows one, also understand instinctively how, at times, to "get right down to business" and how to be precise enough when it is necessary – but only when necessary, not all the time. In so doing, they are instinctively implementing **the precision-imprecision alternance, which is wholly part of life and without which life becomes unbearable**.

So many people say that they can no longer remember names, yet they never forget the person's face, what they stood for, or their striking ideas, as the case may be. So, they tell themselves that memory fades with age, as the used-up brain cells disappear. From this comes the notion that memory-loss has to be accepted as one of the handicaps of old age. I have seen many, many patients resign themselves to this without ever wondering if this was not more a question of life taking on a new orientation with memory also taking its part in the transformation, no longer retaining the same things in the same old way.

Not to be obsessed with precision when there is no need for it, when things can flow perfectly well without it, and to understand precision is meant to alternate naturally with moments of imprecision can be very useful for a certain type of person usually called a "perfectionist". They can also be helped by realizing that during moments of imprecision one rests and things suddenly sort themselves out because they are flowing better. As a doctor, it has often been my lot to help throw some light on the situation of those who suffer from being told in all sorts of different ways: "Why don't you stop being such a perfectionist!" This reproach makes them very unhappy or, at least, uncomfortable because their genius lies in precisely that: perfectionism.

I explain to them that perfectionism is a positive quality but that we need to know how to alternate it with imprecision and casualness, especially when things are not worth the bother or when they more naturally belong to the hazy and the vague. This advice generally helped them to make real progress, for it allowed them to use their brilliance as an asset and no longer view it as a fault.

"Spare your perfectionist drive and concentration for the things and the times that will require them. See how much, then, you will be appreciated if you go to work in a precision explosives factory. But once outside, leave it behind. Leave others to live how they see fit." Setting their natural inclination into this new framework, in well-lived-out and welcomed alternance, generally did people much good.

If you have a rounder personality and you rather like the vagueness in which you feel quite at ease, think about taking little opportunities to be precise at times. It will provoke an alternance which can benefit you considerably: The world of precision will no longer represent something unknown or threatening for you.

If, on the other hand, you are a pointed person, even for little things, then notice those vague and imprecise moments in passing as a chance to live a little differently and aerate your fastidious personality. There is no danger in doing so and it will likely do you a lot of good.

"Always Be Positive:" A Big Mistake

With some thirty years lag behind the United States, the slogans "Be positive" and "Don't look at the negative side of things" were let loose on France in the 1980s. It started with the story of the half-full, half-empty bottle of wine that two tramps discover at the same time. One, an optimist, jumps with joy at the thought that it is half-full. The other, a pessimist, moans because it is already half-empty. Then they have a good laugh at each other. The moral: We might as well be "always positive" and see only the good side of things.

Believing that one has to always be positive can manifest itself in that appalling smile (called the "commercial smile") which is so awful because it is fixed, giving rise to the question whether anything true remains in the countenance. It is like the neons and spotlights which are installed not to illuminate but to dazzle, to stop one thinking and to get one to the cash desk before having an opportunity to reason things out.

This ever-false, always-positive smile lacks correspondence with anything natural inside people, who are made up of moods and the ups and downs which form the very substance of life. Nobody can be totally and at all times positive. The idea is stupid, unbalancing, and false. In all my life as a doctor in direct contact with the reality of people's lives, I have never come across one instance of it being true.

There are high-points: when thoughts and reactions are very positive. These are periods of crescendo, the crest of the wave, the high tide. And there are low-points: when thoughts are negative and destructive and one is at a "low ebb", as the natural and very expressive saying goes.

It is very important not to fake those highs and put on a smile when one has an overwhelming longing to cry. Crying will give one authenticity in return. To lie to oneself and by-pass one's own reality of the moment is catastrophic. It throws one out of phase and someone "out of phase" is no longer in phase with the swinging of their internal clock's pendulum.

Here once more is the fundamental key in alternance – the fact that the trough of the wave must follow the crest. It is vital to know that life is like this and to have the calm certainty that no life is totally positive.

It is idiotic and a swindle to teach "always be positive", for it is, on the contrary, by accepting and living authentically through life's troughs that we profit the most from these difficult learning experiences. Of course, they will make us grind our teeth and cry sometimes and, yes, they are "negative" because they could not be anything other than negative because that is precisely the way in which one experiences them – that is simply the reality of it.

On the other hand, it should be remembered, as experience and observation demonstrate, that a swell in a wave must necessarily be followed by a trough. Just as with the movements of the ocean, this is a natural law, provided we do not let things get into a state of inertia, letting ourselves drift into passive tears and waiting for things to sort themselves out as if by magic, without making any of the effort implicitly required by moments of crisis or depression.

You feel yourself sinking right to the bottom; don't try to swim against the waves; don't force yourself to smile no matter what and see the positive side of things, the half-full bottle. In that very moment your life is totally dramatic. Its only positive aspect is the fact that you are alive and still able to breathe, to survive. So be unhappy and cry, for however long the wave of grief or disappointment remains within you – and work, work, work without respite.

If you cannot manage to work and are stunned by it all, then turn to the "alternance reflex": change activities, change context and shift to something opposite. Make an effort not to smile like an imbecile or a liar when you are sad or depressed but to discover how to alternate, how to "take a break", how to get your breath back, and then rise back up normally and with ease on the wave of life.

In some cases we cannot, by ourselves, manage to find the way to get this breath back and rise up but we can turn to others for the help they can bring. Believers can look to heaven and turn to God. Before God, they can at last cry and express the whole of their grief. One is no longer obliged to be "positive".

Alternance and the Essential Feminine

Whereas men generally need to consciously learn to alternate, women tend to do it instinctually, out of their naturally more alive and developed sense of intuition.

Ideally, a human being can discover a basic alternance between their masculine and feminine polarities, which we all have within. We might even see this in the commandment: Honor thy Mother and Father. The "Mother" being the feminine principle in all its manifestations and the "Father" being the masculine principle in its various characterizations. The defining and fundamental characteristics of these two poles are paramount questions of our time, ones which are perhaps inextricably bound up with our subjective conditioning.

It does appear that women have remained closer to nature, with their fundamental instinct of conversing on the physical level which more readily puts them in touch with the rhythms of nature; with these more ingrained, as it were, they are more able to alternate intuitively. Because women have not had to enter so deeply in the world, they have remained closer to the spiritual world, being traditionally less pressured and distracted by the demands of the workplace and, as some spiritual traditions have it, less sullied by it. In the Jewish Orthodox tradition, on Friday night before the Sabbath commences, it is the custom that the men only must undergo the *mikvak*, a purification ritual, to remove the accumulated experience of the world over the week. This is not necessary for the woman.

Men, on the other hand, are generally more tied to the man-made world of reason and analytic intellectuality, the logic of which proceeds linearly, cause and effect being on the same horizontal plane. This analytical logic has maximized productivity, economically speaking, but without conservation of being – thus we witness both the inconvenience of machines and also the consequences to the environment.

Generally speaking, and this means it is not true in all cases, men have developed and use more their left brain hemisphere while women favor their right hemisphere and, as mentioned elsewhere throughout this book, the latter is more conducive to alternance while the former is not.

The psychology of women in different cultures has some general characteristics in common which are known by therapists and psychologists to be notoriously different from those of men – the degree to which these reflect intrinsic psychological differences or societal conditions is a perennial question. The observed result is that true understanding and genuine communication between the sexes is difficult without first undertaking serious work on oneself. In the context of this well-known "battle of the sexes", men are apt to refer to "the baffling and whimsical nature of women". With the insight and perspective of alternance, this can be understood easily by the fact that women tend to naturally alternate much more than men – and this facility with alternance may even baffle them both!

In a woman's everyday life there are typically many alternances:

- the waxing and waning of moods, changes of feelings, less linearity of emotional energies. What's the proverb about a woman's prerogative is to change her mind? This could well be alternance in action.

- the day to day care of others – children, husband, perhaps other dependents. The swings of the pendulum go here from a complete self-sacrificing to self-recollection; to alternate from total giving is to replenish the source of that giving and this can be found in periods of retreat and recharging, in the ways each can feel is needed to give to the self.

- women are still generally responsible for housework and so the clean/dirty alternance and tidy/messy one are significant for them. A great freedom from the mental compulsion of fastidiousness and the terror of perpetual disarray can be gained in reading the chapters on Order and Disorder (Chapters 14 and 15).

- the sense of responsibility can be overwhelming for women today and they desperately need to know how to play! Mothers have a great opportunity to enter into the play of their children, if they can suspend the ever-present needs of housework, meals, laundry, their own work, etc. Men in many ways have still retained a link to this world of play, with its total immersion and singular fascinations. There is a healthy alternance going on when one sees a parent with their child and spontaneously exclaims: "Who is the child and who is the parent here?"

- the alternance of power is very real for women today and each woman can see in her life whether there is a healthy swing between being the master of some situations and being a servant in others. Not getting stuck in either of the endpoints of the alternating pendulum means not having to be always in control in all facets of existence or, the other side, not needing to have all one's decisions made by others.

- conscious awareness of what is objective and what is subjective, and when one is being objective and scientific and when one is voicing opinion or being imaginative is an alternance more women are coming to appreciate. It does not denigrate intuition and imagination to try to find the logical steps which lead to it. Indeed, the wedding of the two – the flash of inspiration and the precise working out of details to materialize it – is the signature of genius.

- women must cope with notions of beauty imposed from the outside, from the all pervasive media, fashion magazines, etc., as well as developing their own relation with their bodies, their own concept of the beautiful. The inner and outer alternance here has many profound aspects: how one integrates the physical and the sensual with the spiritual and ascetical. It is also the alternating rhythms of different periods of life – both for men and women – which may in one period emphasize one rather than the other.

Of course, the list could continue and each can find their personal examples. We can also witness and observe how women alternate, both in their being and in their actions – that is, structurally and functionally, much more than men. This may explain, also, why it is that, on the whole, women seem to recuperate faster then men and why they are more able to tolerate pain and frustration.

The capacity and facility for vitality and aliveness, though, is accessible to all who are in touch with the essential feminine in their being. It is no more the preserve of women than rationality or analytic thinking is the preserve of men. While it is our task and our, sometimes confounding, pleasure to discover the uniqueness of our sex, and perhaps to ponder why we have been born male or female at this particular juncture in human evolution, above us in the sphere of the angels, it is said, androgyny reigns. The retarding forces in evolution would move us back in the direction of the animal level, where the differences of sex are often so pronounced. The forward thrust of evolution would be, then, moving towards the higher spheres.

To conclude, I would like to relate an experience (names have been changed, naturally) which can illustrate how women do alternate, sometimes to the perplexity of the men who love them:

Paul and Jane had been going together for about two years and had a good relationship. They were planning a life together and had meaningful and exciting projects in common, but there was one dark cloud hovering over them, at least for Paul. This is what he finally chose to discuss with me, being as we are good friends.

"I love Jane very much and know she loves me too," Paul said. "But I fear she might be a little crazy and not quite 'together', and this does concern me."

"Many men I know feel the woman they love is a little crazy," I replied. "Tell me why you feel that way and, maybe, together we can gather some insight in your situation."

"Well," said Paul, "at times she tells me that she loves me passionately and cannot live without me. At other times, however, she says that she cannot live with me, that she has to get away, that she will marry someone else. At times she gets very angry with me, telling me I have 'ice in my heart' and don't really care about her because I don't make physical advances to her right then and there. At other times, when I do make advances to her, she becomes cold and indignant, accusing me of being a satyr.

"At times, she spends hours cleaning the house and setting everything in order while, at other times, she makes incredible messes and complains that I am 'insensitive' and 'obsessive-compulsive' if I ask her to be a little more orderly!

"She can be incredibly rational and systematic in her thinking while, at other times, she becomes a new age guru, taking her own subjective and imaginative opinions for invariable and unfailing natural laws. Her moods and emotions also go up and down in roller-coaster fashion: she is, in turn, excited and alive, then calm and 'dead', hot and cold, happy and depressed, loving me, life, and the whole of creation, then hating herself, me, and everything else.

"What is the matter with this woman? Who and what is she **really**? Will the real Jane ever come out? Why can't she be coherent, one way or the other, as I am? I am really concerned that this type of frequent oscillation, irrationality, and flightiness means that she is crazy.''

I drew on my pipe and waited a little before answering. ''Well, Paul, maybe she is all of these things; maybe she is not linear or 'coherent' as you are; maybe she is an alternating being. Have you ever heard of alternance? It's a life-process that can shed some light on your situation because it shows that Jane is not at all 'crazy' but is, functionally and structurally, alternating. It's a very healthy and life-enhancing process . . . Let me tell you about it . . . ''

Slipping into the Wave

One can well imagine the historical sequence of human development. In the beginning there was instinct, which became progressively more and more refined. Over the course of time, humans became the first creatures capable of transmitting the heritage of their past and its experiences. Rituals, ceremonies, and tradition also became part of this transmission; these allowed, in the life of symbol and gesture, some continuity with the instinctual which civilization increasingly ran the risk of losing or forgetting. This story ends, finally, with intuition, the most accomplished stage of human mental activity. As Henry Bergson said, "Intuition is instinct which has become conscious and free."

To cut oneself off from tradition and ritual (often rejected now as being of little use) is to risk cutting oneself off from one's instincts. We thus also run the risk of severing the last fiber of our umbilical cord to the past and of destroying one of the fundamental facets of alternance.

This may be one of the reasons why some have a frantic quest to rediscover rituals and to devote themselves to ancient practices. Perhaps they feel, unconsciously, that this opens up the way to re-finding their roots and retrieving their instinctive sensitivity, at present forgotten or atrophied.

In fact, it has often been noticed that powerful, organic techniques for re-balancing oneself – whether on a physical or psychic level – existed within ancient religious rites or in certain traditional habits.

The same holds true for monastic life. In spite of the considerable imbalances that could be brought about by extensive prayer and meditation, the monk's day was generally balanced out, his life being ordered to bring into play complementary activities indispensable to its overall harmony. The rules laid down by St. Benedict are a striking example of this. They set up a cycle of prayer, meditation, physical work, and human relationships; individual activities and group activities.

Note that all of these constitute very obvious alternances – so neatly that one could have said in this book, from its first pages:

"If you would really like the opportunity to rediscover some of your instinct, to re-activate your intuition, and to live in a more balanced way but have no particular inclination to adopt, say, St. Benedict's rules or the ancestral rituals of this or that traditional system, then, at least, apply the simple and elementary rule of alternance; it is one of the fundamental rhythms of those rituals."

To go into a church or temple to gather your thoughts, pray, or meditate, leaving the social whirlwind for a while is an alternance. When you let yourself perform the non-habitual gestures of a ritual, the roots of which are plunged in a far-off past, that too is an alternance with respect to your daily habits. When you come to the point of asking yourself metaphysical or religious questions in the heart of the modern world's material dialectic – that is an alternance as well.

Anything which momentarily cuts you off from one habitual way of living, acting, or thinking and leads you **momentarily** into something else, that is an alternance. It is one of the ways to rediscover old and rusty instruments which often demand no more than that they be retuned or allowed to find again their elasticity and their range of possibilities.

This is something often sensed by initiates who gain access to new practices. However, later, though boosted by a promising debut, they often get stuck within their rituals or their sect and make an obsession or fixation of it. In part, they break alternance, not realizing that it was that which had been instrumental for them in the first place.

The sacred fire cannot be grasped by speech or silence alone. One needs the interplay of both speech and silence and that is a tradition as old as the world itself. Furthermore, as far as this particular silence/speech alternance is concerned, a therapist is someone who at times must listen and who at times must speak.

Freudian psychoanalysis can be miraculous in its initial week or month because it brings an alternance to those who, in general, have never before had the chance to express themselves that freely. For the first time in their lives, they are faced with someone who listens to them. The power of novelty also comes into play here.

Alternance with respect to something else – it is always so beautiful and joyful at the beginning! Then one falls into entropy, because one is no longer alternating.

Some people find improvement by going from one therapist to another. They think that one is better than another, and this indeed may be the case, but it is rarely the whole story: it may be that changing has simply secured them a needed alternance.

The balance between theory and practice is also a form of alternance.

When one says "do three things at the same time," the phrase itself is at fault. It is really a question of three things done not at the same time but alternately. The ambivalence comes inasmuch as one would *like* to do three things at the same time.

Some people, for example, always feel like being somewhere other than where they are: it is a psychiatric illness. They are ambivalent and therein lies the danger. They are advised to "concentrate on one thing" but it is not the concentration itself that brings their improvement. The improvement comes because their concentration on one point stops the ambivalence, thereby giving them the possibility to alternate. What they do, effectively, is to anchor themselves to one place and, in so doing, disentangle themselves from the other one. They are no longer in two places at once.

Good fortune/bad fortune: part of the waves of life. When things go badly, it is not bad fortune installing itself for good, it is just a low ebb through which one is passing. One should not try to rise up by swimming against the wave. Rather, one can just wait for the surge while swimming with the current.

The technical touch and "the green thumb": the technical hand is rational and calculating, the green thumb is intuitive. One often sees the latter in the case of traditional farmers who farm the same land generation after generation.

To have a "green thumb" corresponds to an inner attitude in which one is receptive to plants and knows their language; it is a whole form of behavior or inner climate. From this one can alternate, being intuitive at certain moments and calculating at others.

Be careful of the "it works now and so it must always work" type of reasoning, for you will get involved with whatever it is and then, one day, it will no longer work – finance, for instance.

There are times in life when one meets all sorts of people on the same wavelength and one almost feels like a star. At other times one feels more like a leper. These correspond to basic alternances at times when the individual needs to re-find his or her self.

If one can manage to say: "It's just a passing moment, a wave in life, an alternance''; or ''This too shall pass away,'' then it is no longer such high drama – and what a help such thoughts are!

Neither ecstasy nor grief extend to infinity, calm yourself! The very fact of realizing that pleasure is temporary can help someone avoid getting stuck in it, wishing to maintain it at all costs, and taking it for granted – all of which will destroy it. One sees this in evenings that one tries to prolong and prolong because they are wonderful: they usually end up in disappointment. One needs to know when to stop.

This is the basic point in the myth of Eros and Psyche. Love dies when one tries to hold onto it. It comes and goes, with highs and lows, and a certain precariousness.

One needs to distinguish between the alternances that one creates and those which one may be aware of but which one has not created, for example, changes in the weather, the tides, the movement of planets . . . Those who fight against these natural forces put themselves in contra-rhythm and fall sick. Do not allow yourself to fight the flow: let yourself slip into the waves of life.

Accept alternances, such as those of pleasure and pain, vitality and fatigue, day and night. Let the day be for thinking and the night for feeling. Some people refuse to sleep and some refuse to wake up: they are always in contra-rhythm or contra-alternance. They get stuck, so tired but refusing to sleep: just go to bed and sleep!

Learn to let go from time to time, let yourself drift even to the point of being negative. To always be positive is a howling imbecility – and a lie.

Another example of alternance is unity and diversity – moments when one turns inwards and moments when one lets off steam.

Here one must distinguish clearly between **alternance** and **change**. Mere change is not really alternance – it is not far-reaching enough. On the other hand, some alternances can go too far. Sometimes one must know how to set limits.

The religions and traditions of ancient societies also have alternances. Carnival time is a fundamental alternance. Germans, sometimes so exacting and austere, live their carnival to the full: they let off steam, doing something different. Wealth and poverty mingle in Brazilian ''Carnival'': the masters become servants and the servants the masters.

Why not treat oneself to a good celebration from time to time, especially when one works very hard on an important project?

Renewing Our Experience of Religious Ritual

Alternance is, although one may not always be conscious of the fact, part of humanity's symphony of instinct. It is also something very present in all of the **main religious traditions**. In former times, following the guidance of this natural instinctive awareness, man **lived his religion integrally**, in a way in which there was a regular alternation in terms of both its structure and function.

However, in the evolution of society towards increased reason and from the unconscious to an ever-larger conscious world perception, man learned to impose his **will**, to master himself, plan his life, and order his thoughts and behavior within a civilization that became more and more urban, industrial, and artificial. It was thus that we lost the vital rhythm of alternance. It is, however, such an essential facet of our basic well-being that we need now to re-establish it in our lives – in ways suggested in this book – but this time it has to be established on a conscious level.

In the calendars, festivals, celebrations, and rituals of the great religions, we can discover – of course, among much else – a whole series of alternances, organized in masterly fashion and with great wisdom. This is particularly the case in Judaism, Islam, and the three main branches of Christianity: the Orthodox, Catholic, and Protestant churches. If one wants to find a way to alternate in life, it does in fact suffice to live according to one's own religion, **integrally and to the full**, though we may be still groping to completely understand all of its deeper reasons and psycho-spiritual expressions.

Let us consider the calendar, holy-days, and liturgy of the Catholic faith. This tapestry is woven of festivals related to the life of Christ and the saints, with each of the festivals bringing to the Catholic a specific mood, a certain change of attitude, a change of activity, a shift from the profane to the sacred, meetings with different people, times to rejoice or weep together, and times to shift from the present to the past or from the present to the future.

On those occasions one gets away from home, from the workplace and the usual daily round, and instead goes to church or, as in some European festivals, onto the streets. One dresses differently, thinks differently, and feels differently, alternating between extroversion and introversion, infraversion and supraversion. One sings, prays, meditates and cries; maybe one changes diet, goes on pilgrimage, or joins a procession.

As for the mass, or liturgy, we can also discover here, amid the inheritance of tradition, a number of alternances: one changes physical position, now sitting, now getting up, now going down on one's knees and, in the Orthodox liturgy, even touching one's head to the ground. One sings, gathers oneself inwardly, responds to the priest's chanted questions and prays, either out loud or inwardly; one gets up to go and receive communion. In these we are setting into use very important functions and "muscles" of consciousness: will (concentration), thought (meditation), feeling (devotion), imagination (visualization) and intuition (invocation-evocation). One focuses on the past (examination of conscience), the present (prayer) and the future (change of attitude and behavior).

There is alternance between **extroversion** (as one follows the mass, meets other people, participates in the chants and responses) and **introversion** (when one gathers the mind within, visualizes and turns to inner prayer). There is also alternance between **infraversion** (orientation towards the physical, sensed, outer world) and **supravision** (orientation towards the psycho-spiritual, supra-sensed world). [These topics are further developed in Peter Roche de Coppens' book *The Nature and Use of Ritual for Spiritual Attainment* published by Llewellyn Publications, St. Paul, Minnesota.]

With the liturgy, events from the life of Christ, His teachings and Passion, as well as current personal, social, and political events are all evoked. Sins are repented and forgiveness is rejoiced in, allowing one to leave church purified, to enter into a "new" life. One shifts from chanting the liturgy to concentration, then to meditation and inner contemplation. One goes from the personal aspect to the inter-personal and the transpersonal, from prayer, ritual, and communion to meeting the priests and other people after the mass. One goes from the outer world into the church, which can be seen as reflecting our psycho-spiritual anatomy and physiology, our "aura", and human consciousness. We then reenter the outer world, feeling relaxed, recharged, purified, and consecrated, ready to once again take up its activities.

These alternances can now become, like the images, symbols, and rituals of the religions in which they are imbedded, more fully conscious, better appreciated, and more deliberately lived.

Alternating Levels of Consciousness

The great spiritual traditions have recommended and practiced fundamental alternance between **work, prayer**, and **recreation**. These alternances, which are structural as well as functional, are concerned with the different activities and levels of our being and life.

Accomplishing concrete actions in the physical world, *work* makes use of body and mind: will, thought, emotion, sensation, and sometimes also imagination and intuition.

Prayer is a mystery transcending our natural functioning, yet on another level prayer makes use of body (position and movement) and mind in an endeavor which has qualities of introversion and supraversion, involving a focus of our attention, thoughts, and feelings on the psycho-spiritual world. The objective is not to accomplish some work which transforms the outer world alone but rather first to transform the inner world of our human consciousness. There is therefore a natural emphasis of external action in the physical world and an initial internal action in the psycho-spiritual world.

Recreation makes use of body and mind to bring about an inner and outer harmonization and "re-creation" of our being and consciousness. It gives priority to play, spontaneity, expression and emotional catharsis.

It is through work that we concentrate our awareness and energies in the physical and socio-cultural world. We incarnate and make real the idealistic vision, by transforming both the world and our own being.

It is through prayer that we direct our awareness, consciousness, and energies towards the spiritual dimensions of being and reality, in order to obtain some "vision" or understanding of what we really are and what we ought to be doing with our lives, and to experience the sacred fire, energy, and motivation that will plunge us back into our origins.

It is through recreation that we manage to discharge all the tensions and stresses built up by our efforts in life for these are always accompanied by powerful inner tensions. We set ourselves back in balance, internally and externally, by integrating within ourselves the extremes of life and form, function and structure.

The above suggests that if we observe what the great spiritual traditions teach and if we practice our own religion – **integrally and thoroughly** – then we will have incorporated into our lives fundamental alternances which can do us a lot of good.

Today science is discovering, slowly but systematically and through personal and reproducible experience, many of the things which the great traditions have offered as experiences but science uses another language. Thus, present day psychology, sociology, and transpersonal anthropology no longer speak of work, prayer, and recreation or of heaven, hell, and purgatory but of extroversion and introversion, of supraversion and infraversion and of the conscious, the supraconscious, and the unconscious.

In practical, working terms, alternance between these levels and orientations is something fundamental. As a general rule, one should never spend more than two or three hours focused on the conscious, logical, and will-based level, without alternating by opening oneself to the supraconscious or the unconscious.

There will normally already exist strong pressures within us urging us to alternate between the ''robot'' and the ''savage'' – as mentioned elsewhere in this book. This is the need to shift from thought and reason to emotion and impulse. What is still missing from that picture is a ''conscious opening'' towards the supraconscious: activating our intuition, ''visions'' and ''revelations'' concerning the higher energies and materials of our being and awareness. This is vital if one is to avoid what Frank Haronian calls ''repression of the sublime'': the negation of and blocking-off of the higher part of our being.

Freud and psychoanalysis have pointed out the consequences and damage brought about by pushing away our instincts and biopsychic impulses. Haronian and Assagioli have shown the essential importance of our supraconscious and the need for it to express itself regularly. Here, we would like to add another step in underlining the fundamental role played by regular alternance between every aspect and level of our being and consciousness, particularly between the supraconscious, the conscious, and the unconscious in our lives.

Example Relevant to This Chapter. (from Peter Roche de Coppens) Here
is how alternance works between the different levels of consciousness
in life:

I am working on a new lecture that I have to give at an
international conference in Montreal in two weeks' time. I do my
research, read the relevant literature, and set out the basic text for my
talk. There has already been alternance in my day, having given a
lecture at the university, taken a long walk, and then done some
Middle Eastern gymnastics. Lunch was with a colleague and some
friends, sharing in the conversation and humor. However, all of
these activities mentioned so far, although alternating, have taken
place solely on a **conscious** plane.

Next I change my awareness center of gravity by shifting it **from
the conscious to the supraconscious**. Comfortably seated in an
armchair, I practice systematic silence throughout the four planes of
my being – the physical, emotional, mental and spiritual. In order to
reach a maximum activation of sensitivity and receptivity, I alternate
between the masculine and feminine polarity of each plane. I then
continue by doing the rituals of the Cross, of the Lord's Prayer and
the Ave Maria, using them as transformers of light, consciousness,
and life. All of my awareness, vital energies, thoughts, and emotions
are directed towards and focused on my psycho–spiritual centers,
which are represented by certain images of light, fire, life and the
expression of transpersonal energies which come down and make
themselves manifest.

My consciousness rises and is transformed. My mind becomes
clear and lucid. New ideas, correspondences and associations
appear. My emotions follow their course, intense and vibrant, and
open up into new feelings. Energies rise and are amplified. I enter
into a new world, filled with energies, thoughts, and emotions which
are, at one and the same time, both subtle and intense –
fundamentally different from those of my "normal" state of
consciousness where the conscious is the main center of gravity.
Refreshed and saturated by the energies and impulses of the
supraconscious, I return to my intellectual work, preparing a chapter
for my next book, but now with enthusiasm and inspiration flowing
freely.

Later in the evening, another fundamental alternance awaits me
for I am going dancing in a new night-club where a different form of
music is being tried out and there is a psychedelic light-show. There
I let myself go, carried by the movements of the dance, the rhythms
of the music and the impulses which flow through my body and

mind. This is the opening-up of the unconscious, the time when biopsychic impulses will bathe my and my partner's being. Lived through like this, for two or three hours, it has a tonic and balancing effect but were it a habit, the focal point of the day, then it might exert an unhealthy influence on my body, consciousness, and life. That which is deadly poisonous in large doses can be a highly-efficient medicine in small doses, when taken at the right moment.

The same goes for certain activities that can be integrated into a rhythm of alternance.

A Day in the Life of Peter Roche de Coppens

6.15 a.m.: The alarm rings – the first alternance of the day – that from sleep to waking. I stretch, trying to do it as well as any cat, and take charge once again of my physical body; not everyone does this – a pity! After stretching, I run through a rapid preview of the day ahead, envisaging the things that ought to be done or that I would like to see accomplished, the people I am due to meet and the tasks allotted me. Stretching is something physical and the day's preview is its mental start-up: so this is another alternance.

There will also be warm room/cold room alternances (my apartment is not uniformly heated). When showering, although I do not go so far as to inflict the rigors of a "Scottish" shower on my body, I do finish off with cold water, even if it simply means splashing a little cold water over myself by hand. This enables me to leave the bathroom not with warm, dilated skin but with a skin cool, fresh and firm, ready to greet the external world.

Here I use a personal technique which I would readily recommend to anyone who felt so inclined: while washing myself with the water, I imagine that I am also cleansing my energy-bodies (vital, emotional and mental) by showering with them with light and spiritual waters.

Next comes meditation/prayer – for me a well-tried way of preparing for the day which is beginning and of launching its emotional and mental processes. Among other things, I invoke the threefold descent of light, fire, and life into my energy bodies, psycho-spiritual centers, and consciousness. I let these impregnate me, invigorate me.

After this comes my moment of silence, using techniques which help me to enter into contact with my deeper being, as well as certain special modes of inner listening. This is my particular way (everyone has their own) of being aware of my four essential levels of being –

physical and vital, emotional, mental and spiritual – and of becoming receptive both to their dynamics and to the alternating harmonizations they suggest to me.

From silence, a form of listening, I move on to theurgy (ritual made up of prayers and key thought-forms). Here, images, symbols, and archetypes come into play, both singly and collectively, as "energy and consciousness transformers". These allow the spiritual energies of light, fire, and life to descend consciously into every part of my being and consciousness (psychospiritual centers, energy-bodies, and psychological functions – thought, feeling, imagination and intuition in particular).

Through every word and every phrase said with all the required attention, with the mind and feeling focused upon a precise image, I am aware of awakenings, activations and setting-in-motion at the level of the head, that of the heart, the shoulders, the hands and feet and finally throughout my entire being. My vibrations, energies and consciousness are heightened; everything starts vibrating, starts pulsating, and that generates tensions, sensations and a life-current which passes through me.

This is my way of bathing in a form of light which is the very source and essence of life, of love, and also of a certain form of knowledge. Finally I re-establish the right sort of connections between my various inner and outer worlds. Then, awakened (a second awakening with respect to that from the night), I feel ready to face my day.

Following this I do what many do: turn on the radio and try and choose some music whose vibrations will penetrate the inner being and awaken good thoughts, good feelings, and good energies, making make me feel like "joining in once more with life's adventure". Then it is time for breakfast, which I prepare myself. I savor it slowly, thinking of all the physical and vital elements entering my body to nourish it, vivify it, and transmute its mineral and vegetable cells which will then be integrated into my physical and psychic being. Next – leave for the university where my classes and students await me.

Since I live only seven minutes' walk away from my office, I go there on foot. (I purposely chose, as a location for my house, a site bordering the campus, the town, and the country.) This provides me with a little walk across the campus, which is half-urban, half countryside. Breathing to the full, I look around me at nature, at life, and at the people waking up and getting ready for their day.

Sometimes I come across a hare or a squirrel, a few birds. I talk to them, making musical and rhythmic sounds, into which goes a lot of feeling and vitality. I "greet" a few plants and trees, look at the sky and reflect upon what I will say to my students. Thus I arrive at my office where I turn on the lights and prepare whatever notes and material will be needed. Sitting in my reclining swivel chair, I proceed to make a list of the targets I have set for the day . . . and this includes "times" and "spaces" for the unexpected and the spontaneous expression of whatever might crop up.

The eight o'clock bell rings. I leave for the classroom where I meet my first students of the day who often are sleepy or "psychically absent". Upon my arrival the class wakes up and attention focuses on the subject at hand.

From eight to ten I have two lectures, separated by a ten-minute break. From ten to eleven I hold a first "office hour". Students come to see me to talk about the course or to discuss the intellectual or sometimes personal questions that are on their minds; this gives me an insight into the deeper domains of their lives. In these moments, the teacher-student roles are inversed: I become their student and they the teacher; they explain various things and give me valuable insights. This process (an excellent form of alternance) is enriching for both of us – remarkably so. It is also the Socratic technique.

Next come the telephone calls so necessary for any sociology teacher who insists on maintaining a permanent update on reality; also the photocopying of articles, book-extracts, and lectures. Then comes my secretary and her work, to see if there are things to be done on that front.

Lunch, around eleven and often in the company of a student, is taken in the cafeteria where one browses in order to choose "instinctively" what one will eat today – similar to some Greek restaurants where one can taste various dishes before making a final choice. Until midday this provides a sort of break. The discussions are of a much lighter nature (chit-chat, new developments of one sort or another, things that have happened in our lives, etc.).

Midday: back to class for the last lecture, which ends at ten to one; then back to the office for a final "office hour" which will end at two. Then I return home, making sure that the return route is a different one where I can look at other landscapes and clear my mind as much as possible after my work at the university.

Once back home, according to how tired I feel, I sleep for a few minutes to switch off for a while. Then I read or write (alternance):

- To read is to have things coming into oneself (input).
- To write is the opposite, to bring things out of oneself (output).

With respect to this work (reading or writing), which is of course intellectual, I am fortunate enough to have the possibility of a major alternance: woods where I can walk and tire myself physically. Often, during these walks, where I "put my mind in my legs", an original or creative idea will unexpectedly crop up. This is because, in such moments, one tunes into that very special aspect of human intelligence known as intuition.

Dinner time comes, bringing the multiple alternances that it can give rise to or make possible. I often invite a friend or colleague. After dinner, we sometimes take a walk on the campus, through town or into the hills, again discussing a host of topics but mainly our current research or school work.

To bring the evening to its close, I go to watch TV at a friend's if there is a good film, or a documentary, or else I set myself to writing a lecture or a chapter of a new work – or maybe I will read a good book until my eyes fill up with lead or I just feel tired. After washing, I go to bed, where I review the day, taking careful note of the things I have done well or done badly and working out how I can continue into the next day, finishing what needs to be finished, and correcting what must be corrected. Then I fall into a normal sleep and pass into the land of angels, where other persons await me – and other adventures . . .

This small example of a day in my Pennsylvanian life contained alternances of both timing and activity. There were a great deal of them, both minor and major: alternances of introversion-extroversion, of supraversion-infraversion, of input and output, of work and leisure, of human relationships; alternance between soft and hard, hot and cold, interior and exterior, focusing and physical, emotional, mental and spiritual activity.

These alternances allowed me to re-charge myself, to trigger my imagination and originality, to relax myself and find stimulation, by touching and nourishing different facets of my life and consciousness. Thereby, I avoided exhaustion, worry, overdoing things, imbalance and devitalization of certain parts of my being. I gave particular emphasis to my meditation/prayer practices with their initial phase of silence, then theurgy and, finally, the reconnection of the second awakening, which the emergence from meditation adds to the ordinary morning awakening.

Note: Some readers may be quite unfamiliar with, and perhaps surprised by, the methods mentioned above or the new domains of consciousness to which they can lead. These are, in fact, techniques currently being adopted by more and more people who want to find some way out of the overwhelming presence of materialism. I should also mention that they constitute one particular branch of my work, since I am a sociology professor specializing in religious sociology, ritual, and mysticism.

Religious sociology is something more widespread in the States than in France and, through my professional work, I am sometimes summoned before the courts as an expert. In a child custody case, for example, where one of the parents belongs to a certain religious sect, I might be asked to help by giving information on that sect's practices.

To Sum Up. A day without applied alternance or with poorly applied alternance would be a day in which I had let myself become monopolized by the requirements of my work or by the over-intruding demands made by acquaintances to do just any old thing for far too long; or else I would have simply done nothing under the illusion that I was resting or "recharging myself". At the end of such a day, I would have been, by contrast to the day I have described, worn out. In effect, a day without alternance would have been without this variety of activities with its changing rhythms. Inside of such rhythms one finds what can be called "the sacred dance of life".

It is up to each one of us to personalize and adapt the principle of alternance to our own consciousness, our inner self, and our life, according to our particular circumstances and needs. This is no prescribed pattern of dance steps; each dancer's sacred dance is unique.

Jacques Pezé: Memos from the Doctor's Desk

Following the account of Peter Roche de Coppens' daily alternances, I will describe, in order to characterize how one can alternate on every level, one of those failure days when I persisted in my efforts to "finish what I'd started", a day in which I effectively refused the alternances that surged up in me or otherwise presented themselves.

"*Finishing what you've started.*" Let us begin with that. It was what I was taught to do by my education, my studies, my parents, and my social up-bringing. I am, of course, an alternating being, as long as I manage to avoid the traps laid in my path by society, by duty, or by plans formulated by others in which relaxation spells do occur but usually in such an anti-alternating way that they become like lead.

Leaden: to suddenly feel crushed by the weight of one's own life and by all that society imposes. This is the sensation I get sometimes, when things persist and drag on, until some change comes along and I can let out a long sigh of relief. Popular common sense is very familiar with those welcome "phews", the long sighs which generally denote that some alternance is at last taking place. Their sense of physiological relief is excellently appropriate.

Even if I do not always alternate as much and as well as I ought to during my own day, I do make others alternate: the patients who call or come in to see me either because they feel blocked or stuck or simply unwell or because they get the impression that their lives are no longer worth living.

In the not too distant past, when I was still a practicing psychiatrist, I would get telephone calls from early morning onwards from patients who felt "there is no point in getting out of bed". This statement was usually followed by accounts comprising all the ills and pains under the sun. My reply was always very simple and always the same: "You want me to carry on being your doctor? OK, then before

I answer your question about the point of getting out of bed, I'm giving you five minutes to get dressed. Then phone me back and we'll see.''

Five minutes later I would give them an itinerary of a couple of miles to travel as quickly as possible. They were to call me back as soon as they got to the landmark indicated. By then 50% of their ills were usually cleared up. They were no longer asking themselves any questions, except when their trip would be over and where they could find a beach to sit down on. They had just – without clearly realizing it – practiced a major alternance: ''When your head is full, let your mind take refuge in your legs.'' Their cure would carry on, over the telephone, by me giving them something complementary to their journey, a task to be done or some precise objective to accomplish.

Coming back to my professional practice, there were, besides these people who saw no point in getting up, all the others, some of whom needed a healthy kick in the pants so that they could accelerate and some of whom needed holding back by the hair to stop them constantly running around and being agitated. To some, who were bursting from over-eating, I had to prescribe a day of strict diet while to others I had to say ''Get yourself a normal meal as quickly as possible, because your new miracle diet is slowly killing you.'' What diversity there has been in the people I have shaken over the telephone and in the ones who visited my office! I have taught them to rediscover natural alternance which, often aided by this marvelous form of medicine which is homeopathy, can really endow them with the ability to reanimate the sleeping or faulty circuits of ''the reacting man''.

In brief, I was putting other people's clocks back together again at a time when I myself, as a young doctor, had still not put the label ''alternance'' on the ensemble of these cases because they still appeared dissimilar to me. I had yet to discover their common denominator: the necessity of bringing their alternance back to life.

To make others alternate is – let's say it very softly – relatively easier than applying the technique to oneself. To say that one helps others alternate is not to explain how one alternates oneself, in one's own existence and own days, which one offers as examples. I'm coming to it.

First one must understand that it would have been impossible for me to set these others oscillating, at the sorts of rhythm and amplitude typical of my clients, without those movements having repercussions on myself. That would be like someone pretending that they could shake a plum tree without they themselves moving.

Besides this, my own life, my own natural inclination, was alternance, with two major facets: manual work and mental work. This is, in fact, the basic Benedictine formula: "Ora et labora".

I can truly say that every day that I was able to do some manual task, to get me away from my essentially mental task of being a doctor, I was very happy. On the other hand, every day that I exceeded the dose and got myself into some manual work that I was bent on finishing, it became a drudge and I ended up being unhappy because of it. Normally that type of activity thoroughly relaxed me, on account of its concrete nature and the fact that, once accomplished, "there was something to show for it."

When, on certain days, I felt myself stickily caught up in some activity and the horizons seemed blocked, one emergency remedy for my condition was often friendship. However, one does not always have a friend close by, just at that moment, and at such times the telephone is the magic wand which makes distance disappear.

I had no idea, at the time, of the considerable help that alternance brings into the lives we lead. Now I realize that it was already being implemented, by use of the telephone. One can actually receive, through the vibrations of another's voice, in real time, this fabulous gift which is friendship. Time has passed yet still today I have not renounced one iota of my admiration for the telephone, which, bringing either friendship or change or fantasy as it may, is more than just a work-tool.

For me, a successful day is one where I "get out of the right side of bed" in the morning, as the popular expression has it, and where I have managed to continue at a rhythm that I intuitively perceive to be right. It's a very funny thing, this "getting out of the right side of bed". For a long time it aroused my doctor's curiosity. Now that I have this phenomenon of alternance in the right perspective, it all fits more clearly: it is a matter of starting out with suppleness and lightness as basic in one's rhythm, and then staying in that mode for the rest of the day.

Getting out of the right side of the bed for me means capturing the whole dynamic of the day in one fell swoop. It is what corresponds, in Peter Roche de Coppens' day, to the day starting well through the meditations and methods that he uses to enter into the right sort of connection with himself and his day to come.

We have all had days in which hitches occur at a certain point and the totally unexpected turns up; then, somehow, these have to be fitted in with everything else. On the other hand, "getting out of the wrong side of bed" is to accept a bad rhythm, by deciding, for example, to pursue something that is obviously not going to work out, by wanting to swim against the current. At such times, one needs to heave heavily on the oars and row, row until one is exhausted.

One can destroy a successful rhythm: all it takes is to "hang around" too long at table or at a friend's or, if visiting someone, to hang on when the essential things have already been said and the time has come to go. To hang around is to let passivity take over and overtake. One no longer seizes developments. Very quickly, nothing is alternating any more. Everything becomes heavy, overrun, and difficult.

You must be thinking, "Get to the point – what about Jacques Pezé's day?" Since, being a doctor, my days are extremely diversified, it would be inconceivable to present a host of details from a typical day and so up to now I have presented some of the more general elements of an average day, the norm. However, there are others:

- crisis days, sometimes very necessary for making headway in certain problems.

- days of delirious enthusiasm, when everything is possible, everything is undertaken, blown forward by the gust which animates me on those days. It inevitably decreases because it cannot gust continually or because some nuisance or something enervating crops up or because there is some official document to be deciphered, processed, and reciphered. The evocative French expression for these enervating things is *casse-pieds* (literally "foot-breakers") and they certainly cripple one's momentum.

- days of hard work which are hyper-structured and where every thing is concrete, argued-out, and sinister – as far as I am concerned, anyway.

- days too when I fly off once again towards some other mirage. "Another one of his utopias", declare those around me. They always advise me, "Don't take on too much!"

However, looking back on things, it was with those utopias where I succeeded the most; in any case it was those that gave me the most pleasure.

I have spoken a lot about my work and little about my family and leisure activities. The family is a whole dimension embodying feelings of harmony which alternate, obviously, with those very real disputes, proving it to have a healthy general dynamism. As for leisure activities, I have none, in the general sense of the term in our "leisure-enhanced society". I have other activities, other passionate interests; moments of doubt too, when I question myself intensely about things. The main thing is that all these form a succession and oscillate from one to another sufficiently well.

In fact, medicine has led me into two other areas which have developed progressively into professional side-lines in their own right. The one is to do with the environment and the other is group communication techniques. Through my medical practice, I discovered the urgent need for protecting our environment. It seemed futile to treat people when elsewhere they were having to live and breathe in a universe which had become unliveable and unbreathable.

As far as group communication techniques are concerned, I was drawn into them as the logical consequence of my environmental reflections, for one individual can do little in this world which has become so complex. It has become necessary to change over from singular personal thought to group exchanges (another alternance). Without a minimum of practical expertise in group method, these exchanges become very difficult. These methods have, for such a long time, been unknown in France and it was this that led me to teach them.

This all evolved to such a point that I have had, in reality, three professional activities: medicine, environmental concern, and groups. It has been an inexhaustible source of alternance.

Early and Late on the Alternating Uptake

Neither Peter's day nor Jacques Pezé's were that extraordinary; just run-of-the-mill days that one might come across anywhere, by the thousand. Viewed from the outside, they may even seem easy; therein lies the trap and the difficulty, mentioned repeatedly in this book.

When viewed from the inside, when each of us manages to practice alternance and not let him or herself be trapped by continuity, or by letting things drift, it is then not so clear-cut. It is a delicate question of dosing rhythms and maintaining the swing.

If one is early with respect to what would be the "ideal alternance" and dashes to get there before it, one falls into the quirks of those who push themselves to such an extent that they give an impression of perpetually trying to catch up with their own center of gravity.

When one delays alternance, one does decide to alternate but too late in the day. The image here is one of people who do things, oh yes, but never at the right time, "people of lead".

"To be at one with our own personal alternance" – therein is the difficulty, the subtlety, and the basic objective.

The case of one who manages these changes and these variations – these alternances – with skill is not outstanding: it is ordinary.

These days, when one is always after the "scoop", the exception, the ideal model projected for us is always a "champ" of some sort – the one who has pushed himself for years in order to be able to run the 100 metres more quickly than anyone else, solely in the hope of one day being the best.

Once our eyes have gotten into the habit of locking onto those who stand out from the crowd, it becomes hard to see the admirable, wholesome, healthy, and exemplary in non-champions. This is the other aspect of the difficulty and, also, the very heart of alternance which consists of perceiving, conceiving-of, and, above all, of living-out the ordinary as something extraordinary and the run-of-the-mill as something uniquely incredible.

Science and Tradition

In our age, in which a growing number of people are seeking to free themselves from narrow, crushing materialism, it is very important that all those capable of illuminating the way – by establishing beacons of reference and by indicating the dangers, limits, and the possibilities – do so. This seems to us to be a new social duty.

Yesterday there was, at least in France, more emphasis on "social concerns", socialism, the quest for men to have equal opportunity. Today, now that this goal has been achieved (sometimes for the better, sometimes for the worse) the targets have been set higher and the goal now is to enable everyone to fulfill their lives, This is a hope felt throughout the world.

For many people, this fulfillment takes place through the various opportunities that now exist for getting away from materialism, provided they avoid the traps of unhealthy mysticism or regressive religiousness, or the fetishes of some magician, charlatan, or guru. Those who are themselves de-structured, for example, must beware of developing a mythical admiration for fake ascetics, or brilliant schizophrenics and paranoics whose own personality is strong and powerfully structuring. In brief, the traps exist and the thread of tradition which used to give one the possibility of situating oneself and finding one's bearings is often no longer there to indicate which ways to follow and which ways to shun.

Tradition: This is another term, another concept, that needs explanation, for there are traps that one might head straight into here. They can be schematically split into two distinct areas: the gooey-eyed vision of a poorly-understood past and the leap forward into neurotic futurism.

It is quite tempting to go back in time and rediscover with delight the things which added balance to the lives of our forefathers or past generations. The temptation is made more dangerous by the past being so eminently reassuring, simply because it has passed and is behind us: all one has to do is to turn back and look.

To leap forward, convinced that one has the gift of second sight and is being invisibly driven, presents another sort of risk or perhaps even a neurotic tendency; that of fleeing forward to escape a present that cannot be dealt with, because it seems too ponderously difficult. We can see this all around us, perhaps even in those whom we know well enough to realize how unhappy and imbalanced this escapism makes them. Well then, what to do?

And what help can science offer, with its certainties, its basic laws: all that is demonstrable and can be reproduced in laboratories?

We will not, here, go into the present quarrels taking place between scientists and those who make a cult of science, where each camp criticizes the other, either for lack of precision on the one hand or for a narrow-minded rigor, on the other, a rigor which leads to refutation of the intangible and as-yet-unmeasurable.

Science and Tradition is, in fact, the title of the series in which this book appears in its French-language edition. So it is to this integrated program that we are contributing this particular and new element, this new perspective. However, one must be aware that this approach does not consist in turning solely to the past nor is it as easy as confidently brandishing a present locked up in a neatly four-sided science.

Science and tradition: those two elements can respond to each other in an echo-like alternation that gives one the benefit of a previously-unknown illumination, shining its light on new paths to be discovered.

We do not want to walk a tightrope here; something that demands the exceptional qualities of the few who edge from one skyscraper to another, instilling the thrill of admiration in the crowd below, while they themselves risk life and limb to test their own limits.

This book, as we have said on several occasions, is not based upon following or copying the examples set by champions. It is not modeled on or for the expert but is written, quite simply, for everyone, in the hope of allowing each individual to progress using the ordinary means at their disposal; then each can discover his own particular art of living, using the illumination he is able to pick up here or there every day.

Science and tradition: the opening-up of intuition, the spiritual inspiration of the past as it combines with the finest approach of the most rigorous scientific method. There again we have a major alternance.

Science works from the bottom up, building on direct observation and living experience. Tradition, on the other hand, comes down ''from above'', from the vision and intuition of those ''inspired'', whether they are saints, prophets, a founder of a new religious or social order, or be they great historical figures who leave their mark upon an age, thus creating and contributing facets of a particular tradition.

Tradition is based upon collective experience, as lived over long periods. Science, however, can emerge in the present through the individual experience of one initiated into its techniques and norms.

Science or Tradition: A Choice?

Advocates of science and advocates of tradition are often seen opposing each other: the debate has become a wide-ranging controversy in the present day. The more conciliatory, or the more open, say that we need both and that both have their purpose – but even that fails to appease the two camps.

Most of us have both of these tendencies and give the one or the other more emphasis according to our inclination. Their imbalance, the lack of the neglected aspect, will often make us feel unhappy and a little amputated. For some people it is an actual source of inner conflict; they accuse themselves, turn by turn, of giving too much credence to the one tendency or the other, their inner conflict reinforced in hearing the same accusations they make of themselves echoed from without by various different social groups.

Once one has properly assimilated and revived the concept of alternance and the natural dynamic swing that it is, this whole issue becomes both simpler and clearer. It is no longer a question of having to choose between science and tradition but of knowing how to shift from one of these two facets of wisdom to the other. One does so according to circumstances in which one happens to be at the time, an inner impulse emanating from one's deeper self, one's intuitive intelligence, or just naturally in accord with one's needs or from a certain environmental sensitivity.

Science and/or Tradition

Curious how the title of the sub-head, with the ''and/or'' now added, makes more sense and takes on a wider meaning. It is, effectively, a way of looking at the world in two simultaneous ways, which co-exist within our complex being.

Instead of opposing either science or tradition in a sterile, stilted, confrontation – as often happens in modern thought which variously pits the rational against the nonrational – we can use the idea of alternance to combine science and tradition constructively, at any moment, according to the swing of our own pendulum. Their combination will bring new resources to us and add new pages to our personal book of wisdom.

The novelty of this technique is that, instead of having the one half of our book of wisdom scientific and the other half a compendium of the traditional and esoteric, the pages will be interleaved into a sole text, quite naturally, according to our pendulum's rhythm and our sensitivity's swing, without there being the slightest conflict. As soon as we possess the key of alternance, we can swing, we can oscillate, very lucidly and with all our mind's dynamism, between the charlatans or enlightened ones and the strictest of scientists. This will no longer bring blushes or mental cramp: no more accusations of opportunism or indecision.

Once we have properly integrated the richness and astounding balance of opposites that alternance affords us, we can then even feel free to plunge deeply into tradition and experience all the upheavals and fundamental instinctive echoes that it can provoke in us. Next, as the wave surges in the opposite direction, we can stick rigidly to science's precision, its strictness, its solid concrete wall. Then we can let ourselves be swept, by the backwash of the counter-wave, once more into tradition. And so on . . .

The richness that this movement brings will astonish those who learn to practice it.

The Way the Exclusive "Or" Has Evolved Into the "And/Or"

We know the extent to which language reflects a community's thought, which it either precedes or follows. Also that **and/or** is a recent invention, if we except Beaumarchais' use of it in the ''Marriage of Figaro''. Even ten years ago one would not have seen it in an article or a book. Authors would have been asked to choose, or perhaps the proof-reader would have just simply crossed one out, thinking it a mistake. Today, the double-meaning, the double-reading, is a must in many circumstances. First one reads the sentence with **and**, then one re-reads it with **or**. Both meanings are correct at the same time.

The first book in this *Science and Tradition* series, produced by the publishers, AIRE of Lausanne, Switzerland, was a treatise on geobiology (*Traité de Géobiologie, Théorie et Pratique*). One major section was entitled "Science, Fact and Tradition".

In reading our concluding chapter here, "Science **and/or** Tradition", some sensitive readers may have felt the **and** and the **or** dissociating or distancing themselves. This is because the famous pendulum of alternance, the subject of this book, has started to swing, to oscillate, between the **and** and the **or**.

Observe for yourselves this very strange phenomenon and notice its repercussions in your own thought-processes. Suddenly you will find yourselves with space, just as if, in this world which sometimes seems shrivelled and dense, or in the midst of a crowd where one sometimes feels like an olive in a jar, you suddenly found a way of getting fresh air, without bothering anyone. You might do this through some simple physical gesture, loosening the shoulders by giving them a series of little gyrations or a sort of life-shiver – something like a dog shaking himself as he comes out of the water.

Such is the joy of alternance, the natural oscillation which gives amplitude to our movements, our thoughts, and our lives.

Science **and** tradition: an addition – but how to add opposites? Science **or** tradition: a choice – but why choose one or the other? Which will take priority?

When one brings alternance into play, letting it come back to life in oneself, one no longer needs to reconcile these opposites in order to add them together. Nor does one need to choose or designate priorities. All that happens, quite straightforwardly, is that a solid, supple, and living tissue is created between:

- the past, with its roots in the abyss-like depths of our psyche, of our instinctive impulses, of our rites and civilization and

- modern times, with science and its objective measurements and laser-precision.

In this age, and more specifically right now in our times, there is an increasingly violent opposition between:

- science, with its precision, on the one hand and

- magic, with its mystery, uncertainty, and unexplained psychic mechanisms, on the other.

Is it best to hold these two in opposition, to make what is sacred ground for the one, off-limits for the other? Or would it be better to reconcile them? Both solutions are unsatisfactory: one is stalemated conflict between adversaries and the other can bring some sort of bland compromise wherein nothing is really expressed to the full. However, all this takes on a different light if one applies – yes, yet again – alternance.

Continuum or Alternance: Two Worlds in Opposition

To be efficient and produce tangible, concrete results is the order of the day in our present world. In order to be efficient and to carry things through to their conclusion and reap the results, not just be paid for one's efforts but receive the proper and corresponding salary, it generally proves necessary for there to be some sort of continuum, some continuous application of effort.

There are those who continuously change their goals, objectives, and thus line of action; they spend their time digging furrows and planting seeds only to see their crops harvested by others. In our society, which has become dense and competitive, everyone is obliged to stay vigilantly involved in their work, to stay close by the tree they have planted.

This tendency to strive after continuity is not just a fashion. It is a necessity: a constant pressure exerted upon us by our society and those around us. To succeed these days, it is necessary to set oneself a target and stick to it:

"Find yourself some goal in life and set about attaining it" is advice often given to adolescents.

"Make your mind up about what you want to do and then stick to that."

"My son and my daughter have now found their vocations in life. At last!" is what one hears parents say as they let out a great sigh of relief.

Alternance, our natural tendency in the past, seems something which no longer quite fits somehow into whole areas of our present life. Whoever preaches the contrary might well be accused of being unrealistic. Social and economic circumstances these days often oblige one to change profession in order to find work; it is generally quite a shock and brings a lot of worry. Understandably so, for the person will likely find him or herself in competition with those who have been in that line of business for a long time and who therefore stand a good chance of being better at it.

It is not true that to be the best in one's speciality implies a sole preoccupation?

It is interesting to inquire into the norms of past civilizations, each with their particular styles of social balance, and to ask ourselves what they tended to do, where they applied their efforts, then compare their societies with our own. One can easily imagine that in the past human life was constantly interrupted by obligatory and natural alternances, the magnitude of which mankind was unable to control. Thus a predominant effort could well have been towards continuity.

It is clear that in their earliest days humans, nourishing themselves with whatever they gathered or hunted, lived surrounded by an almost unbelievable accumulation of alternances. They might have dreamt, amid those unceasing discontinuities, of a world which was continuous and stable. It must only have been their gods, rituals, and traditions which represented, for them, some platform or reference point which might lead towards blessed continuity.

In fact, much human effort throughout his history has been determinedly channeled into mastering the weather and the risks it brings. However, the mighty forces of nature, imposing their rhythms and imperturbable cycles, their tempests and eruptions, have always proved the more powerful.

Escaping the imposed day/night rhythm with the invention of the torch and then the candle must have seemed an enormous victory for early mankind, bringing a revolution to life at the time.

The Romans, having absorbed the Greek culture, forged their power through organization, rules, order, continuity in effort, and singularity of technique. But then the Roman empire gradually disintegrated into a worn out system solely trying to perpetuate itself and survive.

We Are Today Manifestly Entering the World of New Imaginations, of Creative Reordering, and of Alternance. Disorder, deconstruction, and rethinking structure – the pundits extol it; centers of creativity are alive with it and teach it.

Imagination – it is the power and magic of our revisioning, the realization of dreams.

But how to court the elusive imagination, live in joyful creativity with her, alternating harmoniously in our fertile disorder, when survival in our society demands the efficiency of the "sole objective" state of mind?

In this complex landscape of inclinations, impulses, obligations, social and economic pressures, and beacons from the past, each of us has to creatively resolve our own unique and not-so-unique problems. Each individual has to work out what to do, how to act, and how, in the most worthwhile way, to use this treasure of vitality, harbored within.

Given the host of methods and techniques proposed to us, some difficult to put into practice and some easy, the varying sorts of medical advice, some more, some less contradictory, and the ancient and modern religions burgeoning around us, alternance constitutes an easy and practical course of action. It allows one to introduce, at every level, in myriad circumstances, consciously and without the slightest guilt, the necessary elements of "a fundamental biological mechanism." Those elements will tend to settle into place by themselves provided that they are not thwarted by fatal habits or overly strong societal pressures.

A minimum of continuum is necessary if we wish to carry out well what we have undertaken. That has to be admitted. There are times when sustained effort and the ideal of perseverance in action can become a heroic feat of willpower. This having been said, alternance is indispensable. Those capable of the incredible sustained efforts themselves know this through experience, through the times when they have let themselves go too far for too long.

There is evidently **not one solution** to this general problem **but elements of a solution**, quite easily understood in terms of this book.

1. First of all, continuity must be viewed as one of the forms of, one of the moments of, alternance: this is of fundamental importance.

2. Following this, given the background of social and economic pressures demanding continuity of us, in one area or another, we need to know how to host alternance impulses occurring within us, without necessarily just waiting for the weekend. Note that weekends have their own special movement – for an alternance that is too regular and predictable merely becomes a mediocre and decadent form of continuity. In contrast, there exist forms of continuity within instability which are likewise mediocre forms of alternance.

3. We should always pick the simplest alternance: the one within the reach of our hand, our body, and our mind.

The essential thing is to alternate. That does not mean achieving something monumental or exemplary; that would only add to the problem of pressure, the fantastic pressures we are already subjected to. Rather it is always possible to introduce small and easy elements of alternance into the continuum.

A striking example of this is to be found in the current trend, in some countries, such as the United States and Japan, of exercise programs or exercise breaks for office workers, in one case for a few minutes out of the hour – when the bell rings. The coffee-corner in a large workspace provides another easy alternance which breaks the continuum.

We can limit the damage done and distortions imposed by continuity in modern life, if we know how to build into it some windows, then lean out of them occasionally and smell the roses.

Then there is that very special way we move our eyelids when, at times, we close them on purpose, then re-open them, declaring to ourselves, to those we love, to the world: "It's not possible! I don't believe my eyes!"

Alternance.

Conclusion

*

By Reanimating Others, You Reanimate Yourself

Reading this book has hopefully given you a new light on certain issues. Whatever your unique personal alternances may already be, you are bound to still find a certain lack, some problems emerging or blocks occurring in getting the rhythm of things right. Do not deplore them or be too shocked. It is normal. Were it otherwise, alternance would never need to be written about in a book such as this.

Remember that this fundamental movement is everywhere, both outside of us and within. Despite its constant presence, the task still remains to re-find, re-animate, and give back to ourselves this lively pendulum. If we do not want to be constantly held back by lack of dynamism, then discovering its vital rhythms becomes a necessity.

Held back – like a magnificent but neglected grandfather clock that is no longer wound for lack of the key, its brass pendulum motionless, suspended, and lifeless. Or it is like the lifelessness of showcase windows, the still display of all the goods of our consumer society, dressed to sell but without soul, without the quirks of nature that we are naturally stimulated by.

This book has tossed you a ball which is going to bounce inside you and around about you for a while. Don't just passively watch this ball. Tap it, keep its motion going yourself. Discover other bounce-rhythms.

And don't forget one thing: by re-animating others, you re-animate yourself. If you do not discover others in this process, then this ball which we have tossed to you will end up by bouncing no longer. It will roll a tiny bit and then stop, ending up in the showcase where it, in turn, will take its place, like a museum-object. Then you will read the label on it:

BOUNCING   BALL

"object designed to bounce when one hits it"

The label will be exact. The physical property will be well described. But there will be no more movement: no bounce.

As is true today for hosts of situations, of objects, and of people – they are "without bounce", as the saying goes. What an image! If **you** want to get "the bouncing ball" out of its showcase and, who knows, help to get others out of theirs, then do not hesitate – do it.

For it is like that that life works.

The Logic of the Unconscious

1. The Logic of the Conscious

Essentially based on reason, the logic of the conscious is that which governs the world in its current visible aspects. Reason and logical reasoning have given rise to some astounding consequences; they have constructed the wonders with which we are so familiar these days – science, electricity, jumbo jets, spaceprobes, etc.

Reason alone, however, is insufficient. Were it sufficient, then how could one ever explain the fact that mankind, all of whose energies are channeled into staying alive, healing sickness and delaying death, periodically throws itself into wars – that reason readily condemns and in which humans kill each other?

One can make similar, incomprehensible, observations about our lives as individuals. School and a host of books have taught us to reason logically, to be reasonable and "aware", yet we are so often quite unreasonable and unaware. Worse, there are certain unreasonable actions which leave an extraordinarily delightful perfume in our memories. As for unconscious actions, some serve as important indications: warnings or signs showing us new ways to follow in our lives.

Well then, ought we to opt for the conscious and all those good reasons for being reasonable and logical? If so, we must bear in mind the fact that a monopoly held by the conscious mind will provoke frightful outbursts from the unconscious, asphyxiated, mind which we might not be able to keep in check.

Perhaps, then, we should favor the unconscious and be ready to accept a certain amount of unreasonable action. Do we not realize the value of the brilliant flashes in which, at times, there manifests an irreplaceable intuition and does this alone not make the unconscious, in the final analysis, the best option?

In fact, there is no need to make a choice: one *or* the other. One needs to find the right time and the right approach for the one *and* the other. Once the unconscious mind is no longer asphyxiated, there is more reason for creating sensational situations to give oneself a break.

It is well-known that the unconscious acts upon the conscious. Indeed that is the very point of most Freudian psychoanalysis; something that has directly concerned millions of people for years now. The contrary, however, is not true: it is difficult for the conscious mind to act upon the unconscious, except to unhinge it. The unconscious has different rhythms and different ways of being accessed than the ones that our logical reasoning imagines.

The conscious/unconscious ensemble is an inter-reacting binomial. Although many of its subtleties are still unknown, observation would suggest that alternance is one of its vital mechanisms. The whole point and aim of this book is to help re-establish this essential mechanism, presently absent or disturbed. Its good functioning is absolutely necessary if we are to increase (and perfect) our ability to hit upon just the right moments and find, in ourselves, just the right ways of tackling things.

2. The Logic of the Unconscious

For a long time, it was called the "illogical". Now one says the "non-logical" to signify more clearly that one is in a realm which bears no correspondence to the classical sort of logical reasoning that we are used to.

The "logic of the unconscious" was discovered by Freud at the beginning of this century. For all the increasing amount of study devoted to it, it remains just as impenetrable and insufficiently known as ever. It is something that is observed rather than clearly explained. It is quite obvious that religion and tradition (which are the end result of observations that have accumulated for centuries) take it very much into account. This book has been built upon this "logic of the unconscious", whatever is known of it.

The great sociologist, Max Weber, has questioned in great depth the evolution and distinctive characteristics of Western civilization. His conclusion was that the fundamental aspect of our civilization was rationalization, that is to say, the development of reason and thought to the detriment of emotion and intuition: logic over the illogical and the conscious over the unconscious. But what were the consequences of this? What was the price?

According to Weber, the major consequence was a systematic acquisition of knowledge leading to power. It has been the means for managing to get all one wants, with ever-increasing rapidity and efficiency, even to the point of having to create artificial or unhealthy needs to satisfy the accelerating pace of acquisition. The price one pays for all of that, is what he calls *Der Entsauberung Der Welt* – "the disenchantment of the world", meaning that the more knowledge and power one possesses, the less things satisfy one. This can even go to the extreme of someone having everything but no longer fancying anything whatsoever: all has lost its savor and any possibility of wonder has vanished. As for happiness, which only love can gain, it is sacrificed for power.

As Pascal taught, "The heart has its reasons that reason knows not." For Jacques Pezé and myself, the unconscious has its reasons that the conscious knows not. Among other things, the unconscious needs to express itself from time to time – in its own turn, in its own way. It also needs to be addressed in a language that touches it. In the necessary alternances that take place between the conscious and the unconscious, between the logical and the non-logical, one must now place more emphasis on the unconscious, in order to correct the imbalance that an overweight reason has brought about.

It is in full knowledge of all this that we have deliberately developed this book in a non-structured way, basing it on the logic of the unconscious rather than on that of the conscious – to try to free the stuck pendulum of our being and to try to introduce a bit of "psychic oxygen."

Our Technical Choices

1. The idea behind our choice of formulating this book in its present form (with a non-logical structure) was the realization that neither of us, and for that matter none of our colleagues, had ever seen the logic of the conscious have a beneficial, balancing, effect on the unconscious, except when applied by a real specialist who treated the case concerned with the most rigorous of technique for some months, sometimes years. That is far from the scope of a book like this, the very aim of which is, on the contrary, to suggest solutions that an individual might apply in daily life.

2. The idea of alternance is that it should be as reliable, simple, solid and useful as a jeep. When you need it, you turn the key in the ignition and it starts. It needs no special apprenticeship.

3. Our conscious minds, our wisdom, are today supersaturated with acquired knowledge, to the point where even more ground is stolen from the unconscious by ''sleep-learning'' (hypnopaedia). It is all the more unbalancing on account of our Western knowledge being, for the most part, located in the realm of formal logic, which has nothing at all to do with the logic of the unconscious. The latter has hardly any ground of expression equivalent to its immensity, when one knows the psyche to be like an iceberg, the conscious being the visible part and the unconscious being the submerged part.

4. Those who have some experience of psychotherapy will know that everyone has their blockages, insufficiencies, and imbalances in the various levels of which their psyche is composed. They will know that the psyche will be, according to whether it is healthy or not, either basically favoring or distorting the different rhythms of life. The

insufficiencies and blockages have to be sought out, met up with and remedied *in situ*. This is up to each individual.

Thus, this book was written to be approached from various angles, corresponding to the needs, rhythms, and intuitions of the moment.

Translator's Postscript

This book, as you will surely have noticed, is not linked to any one specific philosophy or religion. Even though I am myself deeply involved with one of our world's great traditions, that of Buddhism (translating its metaphysical texts from the Tibetan language and leading seminars on Buddhist philosophy), I have truly appreciated translating Dr. Pezé and Dr. Roche de Coppens' work on alternance from the French into English. I feel it to be a very valuable and necessary contribution to our modern times.

These decades preceding the twenty-first century will probably determine the future of mankind and this planet. Whatever steps we take now or in the immediate future are and will be guided by our understanding and so any direct contribution, such as this book, which broadens and deepens the popular understanding, leading it towards the natural and common-sense, must be given a truly heartfelt welcome.

In Buddhist ethics, one avoids trying to forcibly change others, either by imposition of will or of philosophy. Aiming to be the perfect friend, always there when needed, one hopes that anything which is wholesome and useful in one's own way of being will eventually be noticed and adopted by others. Of course, when asked, one is always happy to share the benefits of one's own experience and understanding. I mention all this because I feel that this book fulfills such a role. The appreciable experience that Jacques Pezé and Peter Roche de Coppens have in their various fields of expertise has been presented in a "fireside" manner, as advice from friends. Without insistence, pressure, or emotional blackmail, it sits preciously and patiently waiting for you the reader to measure its worth and realize its value to you.

In teaching meditation and metaphysics, one becomes aware of the fact that no technique of philosophical statement is good for everyone. We are all so very, very different and in need of different forms of guidance at different stages in our evolution. This always makes me think of "all the roads that lead to Rome." Rome may be one but the roads and the landscapes that the different travelers cross in order to get there are so beautifully and necessarily varied. For this reason, Buddhist practice is tailored to the individual while Buddhist philosophy mentions the things which are universally true within that spectrum of individual diversity. Alternance has been presented in this book as such a universal. Rather than giving precise techniques which each reader would be obliged to follow, in spite of their individuality, Jacques and Peter have sketched the very character of alternance, leaving each of us to adapt it to our own lives and our individuality.

As for alternance itself, how does it tally with Buddhist thought? One of the basic teachings of Buddhism is that of impermanence. Through studying it, we learn to discover how everything changes all the time, from the never-static molecules of the physical world to never-static activity of our conscious or unconscious mind. Much of the purpose of meditation is to undo the unnecessary knots of illusion that have been tied into our basic way of being by habits harmful to both ourselves and harmful to others.

The main character of those habits is to make us ignore the ever-changing, vast, and magnificent world which is presenting itself every second to our consciousness and intelligence: instead we rest within a dead, pre-formed subjective image of things, built up by conditioning. This study of these habits and how to change them is, of course, something extensive and very meaningful, too big to enter into here. However, I would like to give one or two examples of the shut-off processes they entail and then tie these in with alternance.

The first moment of human love is one powerful example. Somehow, in that moment, one goes beyond the shell of one's usual habits of being and becomes aware of another person's existence. The freshness of un-conditioned awareness is there in all its magnificent beauty. The freshness that is characteristic of alternance. It opens our heart and brings a tremendous wave of freshness into our lives. However, what usually happens, through familiarity, is that one progressively becomes much less aware of the other person, as truly present, and instead retires back into one's shell to relate a great deal of the time to one's own subjective mental picture of that person; the mental cartoon, the limited caricature, instead.

Another example of replacing reality with subjective precon-
ception is that of trying to identify a person, arriving from afar. At
first all of one's senses are alert; the intelligence too. One looks,
listens, and it is all very vivid. But from the moment that
identification takes place – "Oh, it's Fred" – the senses are all turned
down and the mental tag – "Fred" replaces the vivid, naked, open
appreciation of the senses.

The process shown in these two examples – of switching off from
the real to rest in stale images – is, in some ways, happening nearly
every second of our life.

Part of liberation then, for a Buddhist, is to free oneself from the
straightjacket of mental tags and prejudice and to enter the ever-fresh
world of what is. To let vivid and natural intelligence, rooted in
healthy intuition, take over from the stifling, pre-programmed
glasses through which we used to see life: borrowed glasses that gave
us a short-sighted vision of life which was always frustrating and
unsatisfying.

Alternance and change are all around us and within us, as Peter
and Jacques say so many times in this book: it is a question of
becoming aware of that fact; of making one's body and life aware of
that fact. From my own experience, I can say in all honesty that those
who move in the direction of such awareness move towards genuine
peace and great compassion, because they are heading towards that
which is the true nature of our entire universe: the good heart of all
existence. By learning to love oneself, through understanding
oneself, one comes to love others by understanding them. By
learning to change oneself, reasonably and intelligently, one acquires
the true knowledge that will, from time to time, serve as excellent
guidance for others.

This book provides elements which will enable one to start this
great work by oneself for, in the end, most people trust themselves
more than anyone else. They still have the intuitive power to "smell
a rat" or recognize goodness when they see it and so will recognize,
sub-consciously, the down-to-earth good sense presented in these
pages. I do not expect that many people will have the time or the
inclination to dive deeply into the theory or practice of Buddhism and
so welcome this work which makes possible, makes available, to so
many people some of the fibers from which the great faiths of our
world are woven.

Kenneth Holmes, Director of Studies,
Kagyu Samye Ling Tibetan Centre,
Scotland. June 1988.

About the Authors

Jacques Pezé was born in Beirut, Lebanon. He studied at the French High School where his father, also Professor of Philosophy at the American University of Beirut, taught philosophy for some twenty years. His classmates represented fifteen or so different religions and nationalities; his mother tongues were French and Arabic. At the age of 19 he came to Paris to study medicine and has lived there since that time, practicing as a homeopathic doctor.

His medical skill was nurtured by the great French homeopaths of the '50s: Drs. Jacob, Noailles, Chiron, Couturier, Rouy, and Dano. In addition, three others have greatly influenced his life as a doctor and researcher:

- J.L. Moréno, the inventor of psychotherapy and psychodrama,
- the mathematician Arnold Kaufmann (best known for his work with Dr. Zadah of the University of California at Berkeley on "fuzzy sets"), and
- Professor Joanon (Paris) who had, for him, the stature of a prophet.

Besides his medical practice, he has become a specialist in group communication techniques, an interest developed in 1960. In 1970, he began to take a very active part in various European movements for agrobiology and ecology.

In the latter domain, following the Versailles congress on Nature and Progress in 1972, he initiated IFOAM (International Federation of Organic Agriculture Movements) along with Lady Balfour and Mary Langmann (UK), Thierry Goldstein (USA), Denis Bourgeois (France), and Kjelle Arman (Sweden). Today over 100 professional organizations and research institutes, representing more than 60 countries, belong to IFOAM.

In 1974 Dr. Pezé, feeling his role as a physician should also be concerned with environmental questions, became one of the pioneers and co-founders of the BEE (Bureau Européen de l'Environnement at Brussels). This gave him an opportunity to document his studies at the EPA (Environmental Protection Agency, Washington D.C.). At about the same time he created, along with the journalist Robert Barrat, the "Union Belliloise" which fought for the conservation of Belle Isle – a magnificent island in southern Brittany – which was threatened with environmental destruction.

He is the present President of the Fondation de Recherche Médicale Homéopathique Hahnemann (Paris-Neuilly) which extends his activity beyond homeopathy into agrobiology and environmental questions by aiding various groups to further their studies in those domains.

Published Works
Le Medecin Generaliste dans la Societe Contemporaine (The General Practitioner in Modern Society) – awarded 1964 medical prize.

La Civilisation Promotionelle (The Bargain Society) written with the mathematician Professor A. Kaufmann's Quadrivium sociological research group. Robert Morel, 1968.

Les Sous-Hommes et des Super-Machines (Sub-humans and Super-machines) with A. Kaufmann. Albin Michel, Paris, 1970.

L'Homeopathie Aujourd'hui (Homeopathy Today) with Dr. Conan-Mériadec, Dr. Rausse and 20 other doctors. De Vecchi, Paris, 1983.

Allo, Docteur? (Hello, Doctor?) with a group of 7 other doctors. Techniced, Paris, 1986.

Traité de Géobiologie, Théorie et Pratique (A Treatise on Geobiology: Theory and Practice) with B. Babonneau, B. Laflèche and R. Martin. Ed. de l'Aire, Lausanne, 1987.

Peter Roche de Coppens was born in Switzerland at Vevey. He received his secondary education first in Switzerland and then in Argentina, continuing his university studies in the United States, Germany, and Canada, graduating with honours from the University of Columbia. Having been awarded, with distinction, a scholarship from the Woodrow Wilson Foundation, he received two research grants enabling him to further his studies at Fordham University where he received his doctorate in sociology in 1972. In 1978 he received an MSW from the University of Montreal with a specialization in humanist psychotherapy. He worked in that field with Pitirin Sorokin at Harvard and then undertook training in psychosynthesis techniques with Roberto Assagioli in Florence.

Peter Roche de Coppens practices psychotherapy using personal and transpersonal techniques of psychosynthesis, interesting himself particularly in existential crises brought on by psychic and spiritual awakening. Parallel to this, he is professor of sociology and anthropology at East Stroudsburg University in Pennsylvania.

In 1980 he was knighted "Knight Commander of Malta". He is a member of the Board of Directors of the International Institute of Integral Human Studies of Montreal, Canada and Vice-President of the U.S. branch. He is a past Field Faculty member of the Humanistic Psychology Institute of San Francisco. He is a Fellow of the American Orthopsychiatric Association and is listed in most standard directories.

A productive writer, the leitmotif for the past 30 years of his life has been the study of spirituality and the investigation and development of spiritual consciousness. In these studies he has travelled widely to meet mystics, scholars, and spiritually awakened people who have provided him with "living models" for his investigations. He also belongs to and holds high offices in several esoteric and spiritual organizations.

Published Works
Ideal Man in Classical Society Pennsylvania State University Press, 1976.

Spiritual Man in the Modern World University Press of America, 1976.

The Nature and Use of Ritual University Press of America, 1977, 1979.

Spiritual Perspective University Press of America, 1980.

Spiritual Perspectives II: The Spiritual Dimension and Implications of Love, Sex and Marriage University Press of America, 1981.

The Nature and Use of Ritual for Spiritual Attainment Llewellyn Publications, 1987.

The Invisible Temple Llewellyn Publications, 1987.

Les Sept Pilliers de la Connaissance Occidentale Sand Editeur, 1987.

Apocalypse Now, the Challenges of Our Times, Llewellyn Publications, 1988.

The Divine Light and Fire, Element, 1992.

The Sociological Adventure, William C. Brown, 1989, Second Edition Kendall-Hunt, 1991.

The Temple Invisible Sand Editeur, 1988.

Lo Sviluppo dell'uomo Nuovo Eta dell'Acquario, Torino. Vol. 1, 1989; vol. 2, 1990; vol. 3, 1991.

Rituali di Alta Magia Edizioni Mediterranee, Roma, 1990.